Empowering Excellence

Other Titles by Jeff Halstead

*Navigating the New Pedagogy: Six Principles
that Transform Teaching*

Empowering Excellence

Creating Positive, Invigorating Classrooms in a Common Core Environment

Jeff Halstead

ROWMAN & LITTLEFIELD
Lanham • Boulder • New York • London

Published by Rowman & Littlefield
A wholly owned subsidiary of The Rowman & Littlefield Publishing Group, Inc.
4501 Forbes Boulevard, Suite 200, Lanham, Maryland 20706
www.rowman.com

16 Carlisle Street, London W1D 3BT, United Kingdom

British Library Cataloguing in Publication Information Available

Library of Congress Cataloging-in-Publication Data

Library of Congress Cataloging-in-Publication Data Available

ISBN 978-1-4758-0984-8 (cloth : alk. paper) -- ISBN 978-1-4758-0985-5 (pbk. : alk. paper) -- ISBN
978-1-4758-0986-2 (electronic)

∞™ The paper used in this publication meets the minimum requirements of American
National Standard for Information Sciences Permanence of Paper for Printed Library
Materials, ANSI/NISO Z39.48-1992.

Printed in the United States of America

This book is dedicated to the loving memory of our beloved son and brother John.

The best part of the Western tradition has included a recognition of and respect for the individual as a living entity. The function of society is to cultivate the individual.

—Joseph Campbell, *The Power of Myth* (page 239)

Contents

Preface

Major changes in pedagogy and theory have prompted educators to rethink and revise many of their past teaching practices, most recently in the form of assessment. The Common Core State Standards in the United States are reshaping the way curriculum is taught and developed. School districts are moving toward grade reporting that reflects the Common Core and common forms of assessment based on these standards.

To the critical, this standardization of expectations parallels the tight regulation of materials necessary to make Henry Ford's assembly line work. Their concern, to some degree, is justified.

To the optimist, though, all this change—if applied with professional wisdom—has the potential to make the great mystery of learning and grading knowable for students. With a knowable path comes empowerment of students.

Making the learning and grading process transparent and knowable for students is the purpose of this book. In classrooms where teachers are applying these concepts, students are progressing impressively through tangible learning targets. They are empowered learners.

The method of teaching and grading described in this book represents a major step ahead in how teachers assess and interact with students in classrooms. It represents a significant shift in thinking:

- away from a system of amassing points to get a grade in a teacher-centered classroom and
- toward a grading method where each score reflects a measurement of student achievement—what the student knows and is able to do (Wormeli 2006, 103)—based on standards for the course in a student-centered classroom.

Likewise, this progressive method of assessment proposes a great shift in the role teachers and professors play in students' lives. This shift is away from teacher-centered assessment and feedback to a student-centered approach. The new approach to grading practices and the adoption of grading based on Common Core State Standards and Next Generation Science Standards (or similar university-level standards) are at its heart. This shift profoundly transforms the way teachers interact, assess, and support their students.

In order to contrast these progressive methods with more traditional practices, chapters (called "shifts") begin with vignettes describing a fictitious teacher named Mrs. Stacey Westerman. She embodies many of the traditional practices that are alive and well in classrooms today. Each chapter then takes educators through a shift in thinking—twelve shifts total—necessary to empower students. Each of the shifts is essential, but they are not sequential.

Many of the examples in this book are based on English language arts— my field of expertise—but these ideas easily transfer to math, science, social studies, art, and other disciplines.

In the face of standardization in many aspects of classroom instruction, the concepts in this book reaffirm the unique role of teachers in our society: teaching is simply the most important act in humanity. The role of teacher can take many forms: mentor; adult-worth-emulating; encouraging coach; and, of course, educator. At its heart, though, teaching is an extremely compassionate act. Great teachers inspire because they are caring people—their students' academic progress *really* matters to them. Their greatness goes beyond excellent technique. These great teachers change lives for the better.

Empowering Excellence, like its companion text *Navigating the New Pedagogy: Six Principles that Transform Teaching*, is written for application at the interface where modern theory plays out in the challenging settings of actual classrooms. This method of teaching endeavors to empower all students and fill them with confidence and hope.

This book is written for those educators who feel it is their duty to positively impact the lives of *all* students in their busy, often overcrowded classrooms.

Acknowledgments

Thanks to Patrick Daisley, Rick Biggerstaff, Cindy McMahan, and Deb Tully for your comments, suggestions, and contributions. To Joey, thank you for your constant love and support. Many thanks to my wife Deb, for our wonderful family, home, and memories. You're my biggest supporter and my best editor. Thanks for twenty-six years of marriage. And to my editor, Tom Koerner—thank you for our continued partnership.

Introduction

Yearly, millions of people around the globe travel from one point to the next so safely that air travel—while unthinkable due to its complexity 120 years ago—is routine today. Air travel represents success in education in mathematics, sciences, and the arts. Look around at our world. The same statement can be made for the cars we drive, the electronics we use, and the appliances we purchase. Our world is equally enriched by the arts: wonderful books, television, drama, painting, and so forth, that change the way we view our world.

Education is what makes the modern world modern. Without this ability to educate and train the next generation, our world would de-evolve quickly.

Yet as we reflect upon the success of modern culture, let us also ponder *what might have been*. For every successful mathematician, there are likely ten or more students who become so stumped and frustrated by this study that they complete their basic high school or college math requirements and then call it quits. Science for some students can be equally daunting. Language arts for others can be frustrating as well. Sometimes this is due to the way subjects are taught. Sometimes it is the class environment. Some large universities have introductory classes made especially rigorous in order to *sort students out*. Let me repeat this: the class is designed to discourage students from continuing in a field of study that they hope might be a future calling.

We've all seen this: teachers or professors who make the standards for getting an A impossibly high; and instructors who hone in on the most microscopic of class details for a final assessment and then give those tests unreasonable values in the final grade. Many classes are designed like obstacle courses where only the strong and fit survive. Stumbling blocks are thrown in students' way. Those who succeed are viewed as the academic version of survival of the fittest—those ready to enter a field.

Yet education need not be that way. In his classic book *The Seven Habits of Highly Effective People*, Stephen Covey talks about *scarcity* and *abundance* mentalities (1990, 219–20). In the scarcity mentality, resources are limited. People are in constant competition against one another. Teamwork is limited. Only the strong survive.

In the abundance mentality, though, opportunities and resources are plentiful. People work together to create great outcomes. Optimism triumphs because the space on top is not artificially limited.

Schools, with their bell curves and tolerance to failure and mediocrity, function very much under a scarcity mentality. Without question, though, this scarcity mentality has resulted in competition that has led to some phenomenal successes in our culture.

Yet what would happen if, rather than limiting and discouraging students, our education institutions functioned in a way to purposefully create an abundance of mathematicians, scientists, writers, entrepreneurs, and artists? What if teaching were conducted so that all students were given the chance to succeed and believe in themselves? What would happen if we had more of an abundance of the kinds of successes we have already achieved? How different would our world look?

Empowering Excellence outlines a pathway for creating an abundance mentality in a classroom. The book is a twelve-step guide about teaching to the Common Core (or similar university standards) in environments rich in encouragement and support. This book will transform the way experienced educators view their students and their teaching practice. It is written for those teachers who believe—or are ready to believe—that the purpose of our profession is to open the door to all students to a life of wonderful opportunities.

Shift 1

Make a Positive First Impression

A long-established social studies teacher, Mrs. Stacey Westerman has a philosophy: don't be overly friendly in the first quarter of school. Her classroom desks are placed in rows; students are assigned places to sit. Mrs. Westerman means business, and she fears a classroom that gets out of control. Therefore, she has students "hit the ground running" by having an assignment due the second day of school. There are no fun icebreakers for this no-nononsense educator.

Motivational speakers have a saying: "You never get a second chance to make a first impression." Think about the truth in this. How many times do people go to a restaurant never to return due to poor service or marginal food? Despite rave reviews from their friends, they remain reluctant to return and give the eatery a second try. Often in life, people get only one chance, one shot to get it right.

On the other hand, think of the many wonderful people who have the knack to make others feel comfortable and accepted upon a first meeting. This could be a new doctor with a warm bedside manner, a concerned sales person who refuses to pressure a purchase, or a stockbroker who, before opening a portfolio, offers to bring a cup of warm coffee or tea before the discussion of finances begins. First impressions matter, and they impact how people react and invest themselves—and choose to learn.

Few places exist where first impressions are more important than in the classroom. From the initial level of attentiveness teachers afford students to how they present their course, those first impressions deeply influence the degree to which students will dedicate themselves to the course of study.

Teachers who want to empower excellence must start their efforts the moment the class begins for the first time. In the empowered classroom, the

1

power is meant to shift from the teacher to reside in the students. This "empowerment" shift takes time to build, though. A positive, uplifting first impression motivates students by encouraging them to learn. It opens the door to empowerment.

Want to give students a hand up in their academics when starting a new term? Start by giving them a handshake. That's right. In *First Days of School*, Harry Wong suggests that teachers should start the new term by introducing themselves to their students and shaking their hands (2009, 104–5). That simple advice can create an immediate bond. Wait by the door of the classroom, and when students arrive the first day of the term, greet them individually. Introduce yourself, ask their names, shake their hands, and welcome them to the course: "Hello, my name is Mr. Jeff Halstead, and I am looking forward to working with you this semester."

Many K–12 students unaccustomed to such a welcoming invitation will be dumbfounded. At this point, teachers have knocked many of their students off balance—and they are ready to fall the instructor's way. Never underestimate the importance of this simple gesture. Students remember it years later.

On future days, continue to welcome students to class in a friendly manner.

Especially during the first meeting, be professional in attire. This communicates immediately a commitment to professionalism. While this is not a call for a dress code or a return to the era of men in suits and ties and women in dresses, it is a request to look professional. Few would feel comfortable trusting a stockbroker, lawyer, or doctor who paraded in wearing jeans and a T-shirt. Teachers need to dress as do these professionals. Teachers are neither students' friends nor their peers. They are young people's mentors and guides into adult life, and they can communicate this by professional dress.

The next step is to welcome students with a nontraditional classroom. Get rid of the straight rows of desks. Innovate with creative desk arrangements. Desks in straight rows speak to rigidity, both in teaching practice and personality. The modus operando of classrooms like these is typically not encouragement; it is motivation through inflexibility and control. When students walk in and see a classroom organized in other than straight rows, they sense that something is different.

This is a similar experience to walking into a stranger's home. The family photos, children's art taped to the refrigerator, and toys scattered along the floor communicate a warm, loving environment. Classroom arrangements communicate teacher's attitudes the same way. Arrangements where desks are organized in horseshoes or circles speak of classrooms set for deep, whole-group discussion. These creative configurations communicate a value for student participation. Desks organized in twos and fours speak of collaborative work and small-group discussion. They show that teamwork will be expected. Even when teachers lecture (which should be infrequently), desks pushed together work well for "turn and talk" times, where students can discuss and generate questions before they share their thinking, work, and discoveries.

Desk arrangements speak immediately to the learning that awaits in the months ahead. While rows of desks speak of teachers being the center of instruction, creative desk arrangements express an offer to students to invest themselves in the learning process, something vital to empowering excellence.

A key ingredient to empowering excellence is transparency of the learning process ahead. If teachers want excellent performance from students, these young people need to know the route to success and that it is attainable for all. Explaining and discussing class performance expectations needs to be done up front. Students need to know the assessment procedures and expectations for assignment deadlines. They should understand clearly how scores are calculated into grades. Present them with the Common Core State Standards (or the course equivalent) that will be used for assessment during learning. Rubrics used to assess these standards might also be given up front as well, although these are most appropriately given in the lessons where these standards will be assessed.

Place expectations for learning in a prominent place; learning targets and standards posted in a very visible location let students know that this classroom is place of learning.

Include students in the creation of classroom expectations where matters like behavior are concerned. This way they have more ownership. Classroom expectations should include the following:

- Statement of mission: Make this an upbeat statement about your expectations in the classroom environment, for example, "My goal is to create a learning environment that is challenging, encouraging, and successful for all";
- Grading scale: Show how final scores are calculated into letter grades;
- Classroom behavioral expectations (some teachers create these expectations jointly with their students);
- Expectations for assignment deadlines/late work policy;
- Makeup work policy due to absences;
- A tardy policy for unexcused tardies; and
- Behavioral expectations during a teacher's absence and when a substitute is present (for grades K–12).

These expectations should be created, printed, shared with students, and posted in the classroom and on the teacher's website. They should be written in language that is as positive and supportive as possible. These expectations and learning targets (standards) should also be presented to parents at open house.

To foster open two-way communication, consider creating a "parking lot" discussion board in your classroom. Students may have questions that need to be addressed or want to make respectful comments without sharing aloud. Parking lots are also excellent places for students to post what is going well for them and what they are enjoying. Have a place for this. One method is to create a parking lot on poster board and leave adhesive notes nearby. Students write their questions or comments on the adhesive notes and place them on the parking lot. The class addresses them when appropriate during learning. Leaving space on a classroom whiteboard can serve the same purpose: open communication.

When students are faced with a difficult task or concept, draw a bull's-eye target in the parking lot and allow students to mark where they are in respect to the learning activity. Those solidly understanding the learning can place a check in the middle of the target, while those with lesser understanding can place a mark farther from the middle. This bull's-eye target allows teachers immediate feedback on how students perceive their learning.

However they are used, parking lots empower students to become part of their own learning.

Recognize the value and individuality of each student from the beginning. While get-to-know-you activities may take time from class up front, they pay big dividends over the course of the class: students work harder for teachers who care for them. Create as much a bond as possible with students up front.

One way to do this is to employ an activity or quick project that allows students to reveal important aspects of their lives. One example is having students create a personal crest, something once posted on medieval homes to communicate to strangers the family that dwelled within. Students use symbols from important aspects of their life to share who they are. The teachers create a crest with four blank quadrants: personal culture (family origins) in the top left; favorite school activities in the top right; favorite activities outside school in the lower left-hand quadrant; and important family members and friends in the lower right-hand quadrant. Copied four to a sheet of printer paper, these blank crests allow students to express who they are. Similar rapport can be built by having students write "Where I'm From" poems and illustrate them with art and photos of themselves. Equally effective is a show-and-tell time where students share a handful of physical objects that define them and their families.

With each of these projects, the teacher shares first his or her example. This humanizes the teacher to his or her students. Next, these projects are shared by students and displayed on the walls, creating a homey feel and a sense of belonging.

Having students share their crests, poems, or possessions with the class need not gobble up a great deal of instructional time. Ten minutes a day for a week is usually enough to cover a large class. But the rewards that come in the form of improved rapport with teachers and fellow students are immeasurable.

Where possible, make the rest of the classroom as inviting as possible. Give the classroom a homey look. Decorate rooms with lamps and carpet samples, for example, and allow students to lounge in this comfortable area when reading or doing group work. Make sure the classroom is arranged for movement and easy access to supplies.

Finally, teachers need to express enthusiasm for the course ahead. A teacher passionate with enthusiasm when introducing a lesson can make all the difference in students' attitudes toward the new learning. Unlike the business world, teachers cannot encourage students through pay incentives. The value of the learning needs to be the carrot. Excellent grades as a payoff certainly motivate many but not all. For the tentative student, though, a teacher enthusiastic about his or her course and expressing a message of "You can do it" can be the motivator to really giving the class a solid try.

On the first day of class, be positive, enthusiastic, and authentic. Let students know that the classroom is a place of growth and a safe harbor from the storms of life. Give students the road map to a successful future. Empowerment means placing the abilities for success *within* students.

Remember, teachers never get a second chance to make a first impression. As they work to empower excellence, positive beginnings are an important first step.

Teach with Passion

Mrs. Stacey Westerman loves American history and feels strongly about its value: those who do not remember the mistakes of the past are doomed to repeat them. From her experience, though, she can count on the enthusiasm of about one-third of her students. At least another third would prefer not to be there at all. She therefore deals positively with those students who are interested in history and tolerates those who don't.

Enthusiasm is contagious. It excites. It energizes. A wellspring for enthusiasm is passion, a deeply held love for something. While enthusiasm can rise and fall, passion is long-term, deeply felt, and life defining.

Most educators have been greatly influenced by passionate teachers and professors. Fenton Duvall, for example, was a legendary Whitworth University history professor, much adored by his students. His passion and love of European history made his classroom lectures feel like childhood story time. To this day, the now deceased Duvall is held in uncompromisingly high regard due to his passion for his content and his devotion to his students. Many departed Duvall's classes *wanting* to become history majors.

Most every educator can cite a teacher or professor who changed the way he or she felt about an area of study. In fact, many educators chose college majors due to the passion of their favorite professors. These influences are so powerful that many teachers endeavor to emulate the great educators in their lives.

Passion is persuasive. It is a subtle invitation. Through their passion, enthusiastic educators give their students the first step toward empowerment by delivering this message: this subject matter has value and is worth investing yourselves in.

Students need to see this *purpose* in understanding the required content and performing the necessary skills. Seeing *purpose* is a critical step toward empowerment. English teachers, for example, communicate the value of poetry by their enthusiastic pursuit of its deeper life-relevant messages. Science teachers show the value of understanding the unseen when they share their enthusiasm for how cells grow and mutate. History teachers show the value of learning from the past by their exuberance in digging up the lessons from past historical events that relate to today.

For empowerment to occur, most students need to *connect* to the class being taught. Sure, there are students who will work to do well either due to their individual initiative or a desire for a superior GPA. In the real world of education, though, many students may not *like* the subjects being taught when they first enter class. While the strategies and attitudes in the previous chapter are effective ways to create positive momentum on day one, passion for a subject is the trim tab that can cause remarkable change in student attitudes over time.

What's a trim tab? In the rudder on giant ships is embedded a smaller rudder—or tab—that can be carefully set—or trimmed—to subtly adjust the course of the large craft. Over the course of days, a small adjustment on the trim tab can dramatically influence the ship's course. In the classroom, passion for subject matter can be that subtle force. Over the course of weeks or months, the message of "this subject matter has worth" can realign student attitudes.

Positive attitudes toward subject matter are critical to empowerment. Students will generally direct their lives only in the direction where they see a desired outcome. Teacher passion *connects* students to their studies and *reveals* purpose. Initial teacher passion and purposeful planning to create an engaging, opening hook generates in students enthusiasm and an inner drive to involve themselves in new learning.

While a powerful movement exists in education today to outfit teachers with scientifically identified effective tips and techniques, teaching itself is very much an art, a very human performance act. In fact, teachers should consider themselves as *actors* or *actresses*, with the classroom being their stage and their duty being to ignite passion in their students as great performers produce passion in their audiences.

Teachers' duty is to produce as much passion as possible in their students daily. What is the source of their energy for being the best teacher they can be when they step onto the classroom stage? Their own passion for the subject matter and learning.

There is no fudging passion. It is the outward expression of love for a subject matter. Passion for learning is the reason we professionals become teachers.

Educators who teach with passion communicate an important message to their students: here is something of value for you. When students see and feel the value, they are moved to act. This action is the first step toward empowering students to pursue excellence.

Build Optimism and Growth Mindsets

Mrs. Stacey Westerman insists upon tight standards with her students. Mrs. Westerman is very up front about what is wrong with their work. She believes that pointing out their problems is the only way students will grow. She knocks points off assignments when students don't do precisely what she asks. In order to create a work ethic in her students, assignments, essays, and projects are penalized for being late, with reduced points or zero credit given for late work.

Mrs. Westerman is confident in her teaching practice because her semester grades typically fall along a bell curve. She has a few As, mostly Bs and Cs, and some of those inevitable Ds and Fs, largely due to missing and late work. These low achievers are easy to spot, experience has taught her. Due to their bad attitudes and poor work ethic, she knows that many of these students are doomed to poor grades the moment they enter her class.

There is no doubt about it: punishment works. It motivates. It prompts action. It keeps people under control.

To view the power of punishment, watch drivers throttle back on their speed to avoid a citation when they see a state trooper parked alongside an interstate highway. Think about the power of the April 15 deadline in American culture. Few want to miss the federal tax deadline and cross the Internal Revenue Service.

Punishment can be effective in classrooms as well. Threaten to knock a letter grade off an assignment for every day it is late—a common practice in classrooms—and most students will have it turned in on time rather than suffer a deduction in points. Don't complete the required number of math problems—even though the concept may be well understood—and the score for that assignment is docked points, and a course grade suffers. Teachers and professors threaten to test over obscure parts of a unit—often without telling students what specifically that material will be—in order to punish students who do not know all the coursework well, regardless of its relative value.

No question, punishment works in education for compliant students. In fact, punitive practices are often a fundamental means for motivating students in a traditional classroom. Teachers clearly outline consequences for not completing the work according to expectations. College choices, careers, and future aspirations may be at stake if class guidelines are not met and a mediocre or poor grade is rendered. Students complete the work and prepare for the test to avoid the negative consequences.

The problem with punishment is that while it motivates, it neither inspires nor empowers—both key ingredients for success. Punishment is an external motivator. Punishment works as long as the shadow of a threat hangs over the potential victim. In addition, punishment does not create that internal locus of control that is essential to success later in life. Someone outside is directing the show. People end up responding because they fear negative consequences, and they will typically only do that as long as the punishment exists. Working under the threat of punishment or reprisal also diminishes people's enthusiasm for a project or task. Reduce the enthusiasm, and the quality of the final project often suffers as well.

In many ways, creating a policy of punishment is an easy path for educators. It gives students a clear message: get out of line and a consequence is rendered. Basically, though, punishment works as a motivator only as long as the threat exists.

What does empower students, though? Passion. Dreams. Goals. The desire to better oneself with relevant learning. Knowing the route to success. These are the better motivators. When course work is tied to aspirations, students opt to work hard in a class because they see its relevance and view it as valuable to their future. When students see that they have a chance to succeed, they give their studies a reasonable shot. Their desire drives their efforts.

We educators thrive on motivated students. They are not only a pleasure to teach; they also brighten our day. These students show up to class on time, study diligently, and complete assignments in a timely fashion to get good scores. They make us feel good about ourselves as professionals. Their good work reflects positively on us, making us feel better about our work.

The most powerful motivator for students is the relevance they see for the content and skills in their lives. They view a course's content as serving as a measurable step toward a college of choice or a future career; they may see a course as bettering themselves as individuals.

Still, one key, critical element determines to what degree students will commit themselves to their studies—and other endeavors in their lives.

THE IMPORTANCE OF OPTIMISM

One factor that is a major contributor to success, whether in real life or in the classroom is optimism. The level of optimism that students have for success in classes greatly determines the effort that they will pour into their studies. If students are optimistic about their chances for success, they will study more diligently, take more risks, and work harder than less optimistic students, who see less chance of their efforts resulting in positive outcomes.

In his national best seller *Learned Optimism*, Martin Seligman talks about the impact of optimism on people's lives. Seligman spent decades researching how a person's "explanatory style"—the manner in which people explain why things happen to themselves—impacts their performance and happiness in life. He created a system for categorizing levels of optimism and pessimism in people's explanatory style. He also researched how the levels of optimism and pessimism in explanatory style impacted performance in life.

Seligman's research found that people with optimistic explanatory styles are healthier, happier, and more successful. They are higher-performing athletes and more successful business people. They are more effective politicians. An optimistic explanatory style—or the lack thereof—determines the degree to which people took risks and how fast they rebounded from setbacks in life.

What Seligman has discovered has tremendous ramifications for educators. "The traditional view of achievement, like the traditional view of depression, needs over hauling," Seligman writes (1991, 13). "Our workplaces and our schools operate on the conventional assumption that success results from a combination of talent and desire. When failure occurs, it is because either talent or desire is missing. But failure also can occur when talent and desire are present in abundance but optimism is missing."

Seligman's research found a profound difference in the explanatory styles of optimists and pessimists: "The defining characteristic of pessimists is that they tend to believe that bad events will last a long time, will undermine everything they do, and are their fault" (4–5).

Rather than seeing an unfortunate event as temporary, pessimists see bad events as being long-term. They believe these events will undermine them. They also shoulder the full blame for them, whether that blame is due or not.

Anyone who listens carefully to outward expressions of student self-explanatory style can hear pessimistic attitudes quickly. "I am no good at math" or "I never was a good writer" (or versions thereof) speak of pessimistic traits. The students are carrying the full blame for their academic challenges. Their language speaks of a long-term problem, something pervasive and hard to change.

Educators also experience students who are talented and able and desire to do well, but something holds them back. For many of these students, their pessimistic explanatory style stands in their way of taking risks and making progress. They become a challenge to motivate.

Optimism, however, looks strikingly different in individuals. Seligman continues, "The optimists, who are confronted with the same hard knocks, think about misfortune in the opposite way. They tend to believe that defeat is just a temporary setback, that its causes are confined to this one case. The optimists believe defeat is not their fault: Circumstances, bad luck, or other people brought it about. Such people are unfazed by defeat. Confronted by a bad situation, they perceive it as a challenge and try harder" (4–5). In an interesting twist, Seligman states, "The optimistic style of explaining good events is the opposite of that used for bad events: It's internal rather than external," meaning the optimists see themselves as the cause of their own success (50).

In contrast to pessimists, optimists see setbacks as temporary. The causes are specific and confined. Unlike their successes, they see bad events as coming from outside them. Bad events roll right off them. After a reasonable time of disappointment over a setback, they are ready to correct their course since they are not weighed down with the burden of carrying the causes of their actions. Nor do these optimists see bad events as long lasting.

While bad things are seen as coming from outside themselves, optimists take full credit for the good things that happen to them. Basically, they are the cause of the good events in their lives. They internalize their success. Bad events are blamed on someone or something else. Their causes are kept at an arm's length.

What Seligman's research suggests makes sense from the classroom perspective. Educators know those students who bounce back from a poor score on a test or an assignment. They may blame the test or say that the teacher didn't cover that topic well in class. Eventually, they ask what needs to be done to get the grades they desire. These students show the traits of optimism: a setback is specific and temporary; they choose to rise to meet the challenge.

Optimistic students also revel in success. They are ready to take full credit for a job well done.

On the other hand, teachers or professors experience students who take less-than-satisfactory scores hard. They stun them. It reduces their enthusiasm for the course. These students show traits of pessimism: the bad event is personalized; it feels long-term, inescapable. Bad events confirm to the pessimists what they already feel about themselves.

Then of course, there are students who don't really choose to try at all. These students are the victims of regular setbacks and have fallen into a submissive state Seligman refers to as "learned helplessness." As Seligman explains, "Learned helplessness is the giving-up reaction, the quitting response that follows from the belief that whatever you do doesn't matter" (15).

Classrooms today are filled with students who range from the optimistic to those terribly pessimistic. Still, hope exists for the less than optimistic. "I have found, however, that pessimism is escapable. Pessimists can in fact learn to be optimists, and not through mindless devices like whistling a happy tune or mouthing platitudes," Seligman writes (5). In his book, he explains that "habits of thinking need not be forever" (8). "Changing the destructive things you say to yourself when you experience setbacks that life deals all of us is the central skill of optimism" (15).

Seligman's book *Learned Optimism* outlines easy-to-follow techniques that have helped thousands of people rise above pessimism, moving them from negative explanatory styles to more optimistic ones. Seligman's techniques, though, take time to implement as regular practice. The change in explanatory style is an ongoing process, something beyond the scope of an educator with dozens and dozens of students to deal with.

Nonetheless, educators can create learning environments that operate under Seligman's principles of optimism. Teachers can help students reframe to operate on an optimistic explanatory by the way they conduct their lessons and deal with students. When students present a pessimistic explanation for their lack of success, teachers can show students how to reframe those negative sentiments with revised self-talk containing an optimistic twist.

When a student receives a poor score on her essay, she may mutter, "Once again I got a poor grade. I am a really lousy writer and English student." The student feels that the problem is permanent and pervasive. The teacher, though, can redirect the student's thinking. "This is the first essay you have completed for my class," the language arts educator might explain. "What brought your grade down are three things that I know how to fix. These are very common issue and skills you can learn. I have done this successfully with students many times." The teacher reframes the challenges the student faces as temporary and solvable. See table 3.1 for other examples of redirecting student thinking.

Educators can redirect thinking to foster learning environments where the challenges students face are viewed as temporary and solvable. Student successes become celebrated.

Showing students the route to an optimistic lifestyle can have a lifelong impact. Not only will these attitudes impact students striving for academic excellence, but also they will build confidence and explanatory style for successful pursuits later in life, such as better health, greater risk taking, and job promotions.

Table 3.1

Student's Comment	Teacher's Redirecting Comments
"Once again I bombed a science test. I'll never be able to understand falling objects."	"Last year a third of my class didn't meet the standard on the concept of terminal velocity when they took their first assessment. All but one met the standard by quarter. You can too."
"Math is not my subject. I'll never be able to understand the concept of rectangular prisms."	"Do you remember your challenges finding the area of a pentagon in the last unit? You told me the same thing then. You got a B on that unit exam. You can come to understand this too."
"I have never done well at history because I can't remember dates."	"Can you tell me the dates of your parents' and sibling's birthdays? [The student gives the teachers those dates.] See, you can remember four right off the top of your head. This tells me that you can remember dates and other facts. I will keep date memorization to a minimum, but like your family birthdates, you can learn to remember these too."
"I can never understand parts of speech."	"You said that same thing to me after the literary devices diagnostic test. You told me that was because you didn't study them in class much last year, so that really wasn't your fault. Remember how hard you worked on your literary devices this year and how well you did? You can do the same for parts of speech."

BUILD GROWTH MINDSETS

Carol Dweck, in her book *Mindset: The New Psychology of Success*, comes to a conclusion similar to Seligman's about different ways of viewing personal capacity. Rather than pessimism and optimism, though, she breaks down capacity into those people who have "fixed mindsets" and those who have "growth mindsets." Many of her observations echo Seligman's.

With fixed mindsets, people believe that little improvement is possible since intellect and talent are thought to be fixed, set permanently. The bell curve is a model for a fixed mindset. No matter what teachers do, a small percentage of students will get As and about the same will get Fs, with the remaining getting Bs to Ds. The idea is that students' fixed intellect and talents, not the teachers' strategies or skills (or lack thereof), are responsible for this bell-curve breakout. Children with fixed mindsets want to make sure they succeed since it validates their intellect or talent. The idea is that smart children should always succeed.

All children start life as exuberant learners: on their own, they learn to walk and talk. Learning is an everyday thing. What puts an end to this exuberant learning? Dweck questions. The fixed mindset. "As soon as children become able to evaluate themselves, some of them become afraid of challenges. They become afraid of not being smart" (16). These individuals take setbacks seriously since they are indicators of unsatisfactory intellect and or talent.

One of the ironies of the concept of IQ is the misconception that it is fixed. While many believe that the IQ test was meant to summarize children's unchangeable intelligence, it was not, Dweck explains. Alfred Binet, a Frenchman working in Paris in the early twentieth century, designed the test to identify children who were not profiting from the Paris public schools, *so that new educational programs could be designed to get them back on track* (Dweck 2008, 5). In no way did Binet consider IQ to be fixed; rather, he saw it as just a measurement of current ability.

This view of intellect and talent as something that can be grown is the basis of the growth mindset. For children with growth mindsets, success is about stretching themselves. It's about becoming smarter (17). With the growth mindset, "people may start with different temperaments and different aptitudes, but it is clear that experience, training and personal effort take them the rest of the way," Dweck writes (5).

This belief in a growth mindset is one core characteristic of excellent educators. "The great teachers believe in the growth of intellect and talent, and they are fascinated with the process of learning," Dweck writes (194). "Teachers with a fixed mindset create an atmosphere of judging. These teachers look at a student's beginning performance and decide who's smart and who's dumb. The give up on the 'dumb' ones. 'They're not *my* responsibility'" (197). Great teachers, on the other hand, set high standards for all their students, not just the ones who are already achieving (196).

Dweck describes how Benjamin Bloom studied 120 world-class concert pianists, sculptors, swimmers, tennis players, mathematicians, and research neurologists. For most of them, their first teachers were incredibly warm and accepting. They created atmospheres of trust, not judgment. The atmosphere was, "I am going to teach you," not "I'm going to judge your talent" (197).

All great teachers teach students *how* to reach high standards. They teach that "there are no shortcuts" and that only hard work will lead to achievement. Growth-minded teachers tell students the truth about their skills and then give the tools to close the gap (198–99).

This concept of a "growth mindset" for both teacher and students is a core principle of *Encouraging Excellence*. If teachers view all students as having the capacity to learn—to build their intellect and talent—then they will create optimistic learning environments where all students will believe they have the capacity to learn and grow. If teachers instruct students in the pathway of the growth mindset, students will work hard, take on challenges, and believe themselves to be filled with great potential.

THE POWER OF ENCOURAGEMENT

Teachers have an incredible power to influence young lives. Their words, gestures, and decisions have the power to uplift students—or to discourage them. Successful adults can recount influential teachers whose kind, supportive words lifted their spirits, gave them hope and self-worth, and even redirected their lives.

With this power comes tremendous responsibility. Teachers and professors can stumble through class time teaching lessons and speaking to students as they may, or these educators can carefully craft a learning environment for students that will benefit their learning, for both the short and the long-term. They can thoughtfully create explanations for success that creates optimism and growth mindsets and undermines pessimism and fixed mindsets in their students.

One of the guiding principles of this book is that excellence cannot be forced. Punitive practices are extrinsic motivators. Excellence—the long-term pursuit of bettering oneself—is an intrinsic pursuit.

Empowering Excellence describes a pathway for creating learning environments that are productive, encouraging, and hopeful. It directs teachers away from the punitive practices of traditional pedagogy toward a classroom philosophy of hope.

Shift 4

Make Grading Meaningful

When the students in Mrs. Westerman's class get back their Friday essay quizzes, they have fractions across the top: 17/25, for example. Point values vary depending upon the number of questions possible. Occasionally, there is a sentence or phrase underlined. Students may even find a check in the margin. If deserved, there is a "Good job" at the top of the paper. After the papers are distributed to students, Mrs. Westerman tells the group what she was looking for in the essays.

Mrs. Westerman prides herself in giving regular weekly essay quizzes, unlike the multiple-choice tests her colleagues typically give their classes.

Essay scores are rising, though. After a few weeks of essay tests, students are finally figuring out what Mrs. Westerman expects from them in order to get good scores on her tests.

One of the great mysteries of life is evaluation. In the business world, employees meet with a supervisor for an assessment of their performance, but workers may leave with little precise feedback that shows them a clear path toward promotion. Telling employees where they fall short and need to improve is a challenging task. It requires tact. Feelings can be hurt.

The field of education is no better. Teachers in many districts can attest to vague, valueless evaluations they receive from their principals or school districts each year. Administrators are wary of placing negative comments on evaluations lest those teachers grieve the action with their union.

Vague grading policies are the classroom equivalent. Students try their hardest to meet a teacher's expectations (versus clear learning targets) only to receive scores and little feedback, which leaves them baffled about what they did right and where they fell short. They have little idea about what steps to take for a better grade. A mysterious gap exists between what they thought the teacher expected and how the teacher actually graded.

Traditionally, grading has been the mystical realm of the teacher or professor. Students are often left powerless by assessment methods. They are kept in the dark. Since each educator teaches different curriculum and grades a little differently, students have to figure out, oftentimes through trial and error, what it takes to get a good grade. In addition, teachers have different levels of expectations. A student getting a B in one course might be awarded an A− for the same work from a different instructor. Some teachers have reputations for being easy graders. Getting an A from another instructor teaching the same course can be considered a badge of honor.

Teachers and professors instructing and grading the same courses with vastly different levels of rigor and expectations is very common. Rather than primarily focusing on academic achievement, though, students spend energy trying to figure out exactly what a teacher or professor expects. Instead of demanding clarity, students often comply, fearing some form of retribution.

Parents who have access to online grade books can attest to wide swings in grading practices and expectations from class to class. Unless schools and school districts have standardized grading policies, these practices can differ greatly between classes. From class to class, different point values are used to calculate work. Different percentages are often used to calculate letter grades from course to course. Parents are confused. The worst part, though, is that students are often left confused by grading.

For education to be empowering, students need to know the pathway to success. For this pathway to be accessible, grading policy and teacher expectations and standards need to be as transparent as possible.

Like sexism and racism, which were once the status quo until they were challenged, grading inequities and injustices have been accepted just because that's the way they are. Voices of reason, like Ken O'Connor, Rick Stiggins, Thomas Guskey, and Rick Wormeli, though, have challenged traditional assessment practices and demanded a knowable path to excellence for students through the use of standards-based instruction and assessment.

AN EVOLUTION IN THINKING

Standards have always existed. They were just inside teacher's minds. Instructors, to the best of their abilities, explained their expectations for the assignments, essays, and projects they assigned. Students dutifully worked to achieve those expectations. When student work was handed back, it came with a score, a percentage, or a fraction on top that represented its assessed quality. Sometimes comments were added relating to the paper. Unless students met individually with teachers or professors, though, they might not fully understand why they scored the way they did. These students didn't always know what they needed to do next to grow.

Still, for all its shortcomings, the system functioned reasonably well for the empowered and privileged student with a fine-tuned sense of inference—just not optimally. For the less engaged and less privileged student, though, the ambiguity could be discouraging.

Certainly, standards existed. What was missing was that students didn't always know clearly what good writing, analysis, or conceptual understanding in content areas looked like.

For K–12 language arts teachers in the 1990s, the small step of adopting the Six Traits of Quality Writing was a giant leap forward for instruction. Previously, teachers typically gave students a holistic grade and comments. With the adoption of these Six Traits, though, teachers presented to students rubrics with categories upon which their writing would be scored: ideas, organization, sentence fluency, word choice, voice, and conventions. Each category was rated on a four-point scale (4 = exemplary; 3 = proficient; 2 = emerging; and 1 = rudimentary) with descriptors identifying the different levels of quality for each of these traits.

When teachers placed checkmarks in the rubrics' boxes and highlighted key wording in the descriptors, students were given a much more concrete idea of where their writing strengths and challenges lay. These descriptors formed the basis for formative feedback about how to improve. Rather than a nebulous "93%/A" or an "83%/B" on a paper, the Six Traits quantified writing expectations and solidified what that grade really meant.

The Six Traits revolutionized the way teachers taught writing and talked to students about how they could improve their skills. (English language arts Common Core State Standards for expository writing bear the indelible stamp of these Six Traits.)

In addition, students could see how checks in Six Traits descriptors evolved into a final score. Rather than trying to figure out the reasoning behind a percentage or fraction, students could see how their actual score was derived. Since the Six Traits removed ambiguity from how writing was scored, these rubrics made grading meaningful for students.

The use of rubrics has evolved to become common practice in other disciplines. Science teachers use them to quantify the outcome for an activity—what a quality lab report looks like, for example. Rubrics appeared in social studies class as a means of communicating learning targets for extended projects. In Washington State, projects called Classroom Based Assessments (CBAs), which were created at the state level by the Office of Superintendent of Public Instruction, have rubrics with carefully articulated descriptors that are tied to the state's standards for learning. Understanding the rubrics is one of the first steps students take in beginning the CBAs. After students read and understand these rubrics, they clearly know the standards of success for the project. Wherever standards need to be assessed, rubrics are needed to communicate key learning targets and how these targets are being scored.

As a result of rubrics, teachers present to students the standards for excellence at the beginning of a task. Students know their learning targets. They can conceptualize what is needed to get the score they desire. These fixed learning targets are key for student performance.

As Rick Stiggins writes in *Classroom Assessment for Student Learning,* "The benefits of clear learning targets are indisputable. When we have a clear vision of where we are headed with students, we communicate that vision to them" (2007, 57). He continues, "Students can hit any target they can see that holds still for them" (59).

Still, rubrics may often be different from classroom to classroom. What are still often missing in making grading meaningful are consistent rubrics and standards from teacher to teacher and school to school. If these standards are different, inevitably so is the outcome across a school system. One student could work his way through a school requesting one set of teachers and receive a very different education from a student who had a different set. Without some consistency, grades lose their meaningfulness.

The next evolution would be to standardize learning outcomes for courses across classrooms, districts, and the state. That means that a student taking an algebra course in Seattle will be held to the same learning standards as the student from Yakima, Washington.

With the adoption of Common Core State Standards (Common Core or CCSS) in English language arts (ELA) and mathematics and the Next Generation Science Standards, academic standards and grading are becoming more consistent from state to state.

What setting mandated standards for each class provides for students is the consistency of a common educational experience in core areas of study. If certain standards must be met for each course, students leave the class with the skills and conceptual understanding necessary for the next course in the series. When the standards are articulated—as they are in the Common Core—students will leave high school with a well-rounded educational experience. There will be no holes in their skills or conceptual understanding. They will be ready for some form of postsecondary education or training. Ideally, education no longer is a hit-and-miss experience, where a quality experience is dependent upon which set of classrooms the students fall into.

The goal of the CCSS is to graduate students prepared for the future with a guaranteed set of skills and solid conceptual understanding in math, reading, and writing articulated in grades K–12.

Grades become meaningful since they are derived from a set of critical, well-articulated standards.

STANDARDS BECOME THE CORE

One of the biggest shifts in thinking for teaching based on standards is the central role standards play in instruction. While this may seem to be an obvious statement, it contrasts strikingly with how classrooms are typically run. For decades, classroom curriculum has often been governed by what chapters in the textbook or which novels should be covered in a grading term. The content drove the curriculum. Units were often organized around themes or concepts: westward expansion in a U.S. history class, acceleration in a physics course, signed numbers in a math class, or realism in a literature study, for example. Covering content, meaning the material in a textbook or novel, was the game. Recall of content was often the outcome teachers sought. Tests were often multiple choice, fill in the blank, matching answer, or true and false.

The emphasis on content was much more relevant in the pre-Internet era, where gathering information was toilsome. In the Google era, students can gather content from their electronic tablets and smartphones; thus, what students should memorize needs to be reprioritized and strategic.

This is not to say that this traditional method of education was without standards. Obviously it was, as explained above. Educators knew what skills and concepts they wanted their students to learn. The problem was that these course standards varied from class to class and school to school, often driven by the chosen curriculum. For example, some language arts teachers may choose to teach some elements of grammar; others may not think it worthy of coverage. As a result, one student may end up with a working understanding of Standard English if he has one set of teachers, where his sister may have little understanding of these important skills if she had classes with a different set of teachers. No "safety net" existed that prevented students from falling through cracks in academic understanding.

What Common Core standards (or a set of similar standards) do is ensure that all students will be exposed to a certain set of language arts skills and concepts for each core course at a grade level throughout a discipline or department. Similarly, in math, concepts are addressed by grade level K–8 and then by conceptual categories in high school. When districts or departments flesh out standards for courses that are not part of the Common Core, they must work to create an articulated web of understanding that ensures students get a well-rounded education, regardless of the teacher or school.

The big shift for teachers, essentially, is that where once novels read and math chapters completed defined the curriculum, in a standards-based environment, the standards are now the curriculum that must be taught to and organized around. Skills and concepts found in the standards are what's assessed—not the volume of instructional content covered.

In language arts, for example, students may read the book *The Great Gatsby* in the English language arts class during their junior year. *Gatsby* is a wonderful, engaging novel that can illuminate the gilded trappings and decadent nature of the Roaring Twenties as well as any history text. Typically, the ELA teacher would certainly discuss the plot, character development, themes, and the historical and real-life lessons students can take from the novel. In fact, traditional practice for assessing *Gatsby* would require students to recall these central characteristics of this work of literature on a test that may contain multiple choice, matching answer, and short and longer essays, most of it recall. Using these methods, the story is the curriculum.

While the study of the novel can remain broad for teaching various aspects of it, what would now actually be assessed—and therefore impact the grade—are a select set of Common Core standards that would be practiced until the student is proficient or better. In the standards-based environment, *Gatsby*, rather than being at the center of study (which it would be in a traditional classroom), becomes a tool to practice and assess skills and conceptual understanding. In fact, a variety of novels could be substituted to meet the same learning targets found in these standards.

When making grading meaningful, three eleventh-grade Common Core ELA standards that could form the basis for the *Gatsby* unit would be the following:

Determine two or more themes or central ideas of a text and analyze their development over the course of the text, including how they interact and build on one another to produce a complex account; provide an objective summary of the text. (English Language Arts, Grades 11 and 12, Key Ideas and Details Standard 2)

Analyze the impact of the author's choices regarding how to develop and relate elements of a story or drama (e.g., where a story is set, how the action is ordered, and how the characters are introduced and developed). (English Language Arts, Grades 11 and 12, Key Ideas and Details Standard 3)

Analyze a case in which grasping point of view requires distinguishing what is directly stated in a text from what is really meant (e.g., satire, sarcasm, irony, or understatement). (English Language Arts, Grades 11 and 12, Craft and Structure Standard 6, p. 38)

Keeping these standards at the forefront, language arts teachers would plan learning activities that would help students grow in their proficiency with each standard. *Gatsby* becomes the tool to meet these standards. In fact, since students do not commonly meet a standard on their first attempt (standards-based first attempts are formative), *Gatsby* might be just *one* of the literary selections used to work on these same standards through the grading term, since students will need multiple opportunities to learn to use these challenging skills proficiently.

Note, too, that these Common Core standards do not demand the skills in isolation without concepts (lower-level Bloom's Taxonomy cognitive demand), which was common in pre-Google traditional teaching. They require students to use their minds to critically think and analyze material (higher-level Bloom's cognitive demand).

This can be a profound shift in thinking for experienced teachers. Educators with years in the classroom are so accustomed to covering content—the first three American historical eras in the first semester, for example—that shifting to a system of assessment based on set skills and conceptual understanding is quite a change. "Covering" content is so ingrained in many educators that they are willing to complete one unit and start the next regardless of the fact that many students are not ready to make the leap.

The second profound shift is that *all students* are expected to meet the course standards. The implications are that students will get multiple opportunities to be measured in required standards. Naturally, all students will not meet a course standard on a first attempt. As a result, teachers must create multiple opportunities within the content for students to practice and be assessed for standards either within the unit or in the grading term. Among those who do meet a standard on their first assessment, they may want additional opportunities at achieving a higher score.

The result is that the standards (skills and conceptual understanding)—not the actual content of the book or textbook—become the curriculum. The content becomes the environment that allows the standards to be practiced and assessed.

For the veteran teacher, this may look like a whole lot of data that need to be added to a grade book and crunched into a final score. First off, not *all* scores need to be added to the grade book. Student work can be assessed, sometimes at the students' desks while they are still completing the task, and valuable feedback can be given. Secondly, Common Core standards can be prioritized. The ELA Common Core standards run through two grade bands, 9–10 for example. Half the Common Core standards can be deemed "power standards" for grade 9 while the remaining standards become "power standards" for grade 10.

When teachers shift to using a grade book where the only scores entered are for standards alone, the jump becomes even greater. In a language arts class, for example, a holistic grade was once given for the entire essay. When grading on standards, separate features of the essay are scored only for the standard(s) the teacher attaches to it. An essay may be scored for only one standard. For example, "Cite strong and thorough textual evidence to support analysis of what the text says explicitly as well as inferences drawn from the text, including determining where the text leaves matters uncertain." Only the quality of elaboration may be assessed in such an essay like this.

Standards-based grading requires a shift in what constitutes homework as well. In a traditional classroom, homework was checked in and given points for completion. Sometimes the points accumulated from practice work outweighed the value of summative assessments, thus skewing the grade. In a standards-based environment, the work is assessed for the standard that is present in the work. Practice work could be assessed as formative work for meeting a standard, with feedback given, yet no grade would be entered in the grade book if the teacher sees that class learning is still at a rudimentary level (remembering that homework should be practice and not new learning). In the traditional method, points were usually given for all work finished.

Five hundred years ago, Copernicus reorganized our view of the universe by placing the sun at its center. Standards do the very same thing in the classroom. They become that body around which everything else is ordered. The role of standards in instruction is reorganizing the way teachers and students view their educational universe as well.

WHAT DO STANDARDS LOOK LIKE? WHAT DO THEY MEAN?

For many K–12 teachers who have plenty of years of classroom experience, the Common Core State Standards look like familiar expectations for their discipline. Teachers may disagree on where particular standards are placed in the curriculum or at which grade level. Teachers may see important components of their current curriculum missing from the Common Core (and thus the name "core," which implies central standards). Still, most Common Core standards look like familiar expectations for learning.

In fact, teachers may find that their process curriculum was much broader than the limited number of Common Core standards attached to a grade level. The idea of the Common Core is not to limit curriculum but to ensure that certain concepts and skills *will be taught*. This should assuage the fears of some who believe that the Common Core will severely limit what they should teach. What the common standards do is require teachers to focus on a set of skills and concepts to make sure they are taught and learned. Across the board, adoption ensures that all students are proficient in the standards. When students are promoted to the next course in the continuum, they are prepared to enter it and do well.

At a first reading, many of the standards appear to be relatively simple to accomplish. The trick, though, is to read the standards carefully and to identify the different levels of requirements. What can look like a simple standard requiring a simple activity can in fact represent the culmination of multiple skills and/or deep conceptual understanding.

For example, Common Core Reading Literature's Key Ideas and Details Standard Number 1 for 9–10 English Language Arts (ELA) reads, "Cite strong and thorough textual evidence to support analysis of what the text says explicitly as well as inferences drawn from the text." Teachers recognize this as a very common activity in an English class. Still, this standard needs to be analyzed (some use the term "unpacked," as if a standard were a piece of luggage that has unknown contents) for the multiple requirements it contains, which are the following:

- Students cite evidence.
- The evidence must be textual.
- The evidence must be strong and thorough.
- The evidence must support the analysis of what the text says explicitly.
- The evidence must support what the students infer about the text.

Teachers who have taught Advanced Placement or Springboard curriculum (both of which originate with the College Board) recognize the prompt as containing a version of Level 1 and Level 2 questioning and thinking. (In Bloom's Taxonomy, these would be Level 1 recall and Level 4 analysis, respectively.)

When the standard asks students to identity what the author says explicitly, they are dealing with Level 1 questioning and thinking: the student looks directly at the text for an answer to a prompt. This is very literal thinking. The student identifies a statement that an author makes in a work of literature. At Level 1, the statement can be pulled directly from the text. The students continue to analyze the text for additional statements that support the author's original statement. Basically, to meet the standard, students would need to analyze the text for a single message supported by several pieces of evidence. At the 9–10 ELA grade level, the evidence must be "strong" and "thorough," meaning the correlations are robust between numerous pieces of text.

For an example of Level 1 thinking, look to the classic, ubiquitously taught novel *To Kill a Mockingbird*. In the novel, Scout is a notorious tomboy. If the teacher were to ask students, "What evidence can be drawn that Scout Finch was a tomboy?" the response can be found literally in the text: she wears overalls rather than a dress to school, she fights boys her age, and she is outspoken and blunt. There is little female polish to this young protagonist. In this case, all the supporting text to the answer is found literally in black and white.

The last phrase in this standard—"as well as inferences drawn from the text"—moves the standard, however, to a much higher level of complexity. For this part of the standard, the activity moves to Level 2, which requires inferential thinking skills. Experienced teachers know that while inference is a skill students use almost minute by minute in their daily lives (analyzing a friend's countenance for her mood, for example), literature can often be subtle in the implications the writers make.

While the Level 1 part of the standard requires students to look for a significant statement (which may appear in as simple a form as a title or a subheading) and then identify robust examples that support the selection, the inference portion—a Level 2 activity—requires almost the opposite. It requires that the student identify numerous text selections and then glean from them what the author is implying in their use.

Any English language arts teacher knows that teaching the skills of inference can be quite challenging with subtle text. The activity needs to be carefully designed if the goal is to get the majority of students to understand what an author is implying.

Again, in *To Kill a Mockingbird*, an excellent example of inference exists. Atticus Finch, the novel's noble protagonist, is a person of uncompromising integrity. In the closing pages of the novel, Sheriff Heck Tate is investigating the death of antagonist Bob Ewell. As a Level 2 question, a teacher might ask, "Read the closing pages of chapter 31 carefully. From the hints given, reconstruct the events that led to Jem's arm being broken, Bob Ewell dying, and Atticus making a choice that runs contrary to his character."

The events of the closing of *Mockingbird* require a relatively high level of inferential thinking skills to take the clues and conclude that it was Boo Radley that killed Bob Ewell and saved Jem Finch since it is *never stated directly*. Further, Atticus is put into a quandary since Sheriff Heck Tate wants to say that Bob Ewell fell on his knife to protect the mentally challenged, deeply reclusive Boo Radley, who actually killed Ewell to protect Jem Finch, Atticus's son. Atticus Finch's integrity calls for all the truth to be shed, but he acquiesces when his daughter Scout recognizes that telling the truth is not the right thing to do. As Scout puts it, telling the truth and exposing the reclusive Boo would "be sort of like shooting a mockingbird, wouldn't it?" It is common for students to struggle with this passage since the text is so subtle. With this example, inferential thinking—Level 2—is the only way to understand the events that close this classic novel.

For grades based on this standard to be meaningful, though, students need to understand the standard's different complexities and how the standard will be scored, preferably through the use of a rubric. This is true of the Common Core or any standard by which students are scored (although the power of the CCSS is that students across America will have their grades derived from common expectations). It is essential that students see the linkage between class standards, how they are scored, and how their scores were derived from these standards. At no time should grading be a mystery if it is to be meaningful.

Those who worry that the Common Core will dictate their entire curriculum need look only to its name: *common core*. These standards are meant to be core standards nationally for all math and language arts classes. Additional standards can be added by school districts. That being said, getting all students to Common Core standards in a grading term is a daunting task. Simply, there are an abundance of standards.

The beauty of the Common Core, once it is in place for years, is that standards build upon one another. Very similar skills were introduced earlier to students in a less rigorous, albeit grade-appropriate form. In a system of articulated standards, the expectations and challenge increase each year, building upon past standards.

For example, the same Key Ideas Reading Standard 1 excerpt for grade 7 reads as follows: "Cite several pieces of textual evidence to support analysis of what the text says explicitly as well as inferences drawn from the text." The standard is nearly identical to the 9–10 standard except for the amount of evidence required. In this standard, it states, "Cite several pieces of textual evidence," as opposed to "Cite strong and thorough textual evidence" for grades 9 and 10 (which required a qualitative approach). The difference is on the level and depth of required support.

The same Key Ideas and Details Standard 1 for grade 5 states, "Quote accurately from a text when explaining what the text says explicitly and when drawing inferences from the text." Note that Level 1 and 2 thinking are a requirement for this standard, although the text must be age appropriate. At this level, though, the emphasis is on the accuracy of citation, not the degree or the depth. This building of the ability to interpret text using inference has been going on for years by the time students enter high school.

In fact, in Key Ideas and Details the term "explicit" first appears in grade 3 and "inference" first appears in grade 4. Still, looking at text to support an answer begins in kindergarten, where Key Ideas and Details Standard 1 directs students to do the following: "With prompting and support, ask and answer questions about key details in a text."

Again, for the standards to become relevant to students, they too need to understand the various levels of complexity that apply to their grade level. This can be accomplished by presenting them with a carefully worded rubric. Learning becomes meaningful when it builds upon past concepts and skills. Students become empowered when ambiguity is replaced with a known pathway to success.

WHEN FAILURE IS NO LONGER FAILURE

With a switch to standards-based instruction, failure is not really failure as long as the student in question has become proficient in *some* of the standards. The correct grade would be "incomplete." Traditionally, minimum success during the school year has been defined as a D or better if the student had enough seat time. Sometimes, it was the lack of daily work that led a capable student to receive a low grade or failure grade. Or teachers passed the student if he or she had good attendance, a good attitude, and did the minimum of work. Summer school or repeating the course was the remedy for failing students as long as they passed this remedial course again with a D or better. Needless to say, this is hardly a way to build excellence for all students since competence was not the measuring stick for advancement.

With a shift to grading based on standards, the standards essentially form the foundation of the curriculum. No longer are teachers worried about which chapters are covered. They are checking their record books to find out which students are meeting the course standards and which are not and therefore need more assistance. There is no longer a question of what students need to know or be able to do for a course.

Currently, about one in five American students does not graduate with their peers, according to the America's Promise Alliance. This statistic is nothing short of staggering. Certainly, if nothing else, a change in assessment methods and a well-articulated pathway back to success is warranted.

The switch to standards-based grading and instruction has the potential to reduce these staggering numbers. When students' grades are based on their performance against course standards, then competency becomes the measurement of success—rather than attendance, seat time, or meaningless homework. Students need to show proficiency in course standards in order to receive class credit.

This is not to argue that attendance or homework is not critical to success in a course. As Rick Wormeli writes in *Fair Isn't Always Equal*, "We know that there is a very high correlation between academic success and effort, behavior and attendance" (2006, 109). Class time spent learning rigorous skills and content—and getting vital feedback from teachers and professors—is crucial to student success. The important thing to remember, though, is that attendance and schoolwork are critical ingredients for success—not success itself. Success is measured by students' ability to meet or exceed standards for the course.

When students do not pass a course, credit retrieval for that course becomes much simpler. In traditional methods, students would have to take the entire course over, completing and resubmitting all assignments again in order to meet the seat-time standards for the course. Summer school is another option.

In a standards-based environment, however, students would only need to repeat the parts of the course where their performance was substandard. For many students, this would mean only a component or two for the course. Students focus on these substandard areas. They apply their efforts to areas of study and knowledge where they need help. When these students show that they meet or exceed a standard for the previously selected substandard areas, then they receive course credit. Competence in skills and conceptual understanding become the measurements by which students pass courses and graduate to more rigorous studies.

CLOSING

By making grading meaningful through the use of rubrics and basing scores on standards, teachers and professors are letting students know precisely how their grades will be calculated. By doing this, they change their relationship with their students. Rather than being a gatekeeper, these educators become more like coaches. They stand side by side in their relationships: students working to achieve course standards and the instructors being at their elbows to assist them. Further, standards-based instruction reduces the stress of grading since both instructors and students know how grades will be calculated. The most important part of making grading meaningful is that it empowers students and gives them a clear pathway to excellence in skills and conceptual understanding they will use for a lifetime.

Shift 5

Build Success — Step-by-Step

Mrs. Westerman tries to build in as much student support as she can into her teaching. Since an American history textbook is her primary resource, and lecture her basic method of teaching, she requires students to take notes while she lectures and answer worksheets when they read. She promises students that the material that will be found on her weekly essay tests can be found on the worksheets and presented in her lectures. To further support students, she allows them to use worksheets and notes when completing their tests.

In the 1840s, tens of thousands of pioneers traveled the two-thousand-mile length of the Oregon Trail for a better life on the West Coast. They walked and rode for months crossing the grasslands of the Great Plains, scaled the Continental Divide through a gap called South Pass, and floated their wagons down the Columbia River. They marked their progress by reaching landmarks like Chimney Rock, Scott's Bluff, and Register Cliff, famous sights and the topics of artists' renditions.

If pioneers had to do their own route finding—as Lewis and Clark's Corps of Discovery had to do—few would have attempted the crossing, and fewer still would have arrived safely at their western destinations. Hired trail guides led the wagon trains west, even when the trail had become well chiseled into the landscape. The trail guides knew how to ford dangerous rivers, double-team wagons to scale steep slopes, and pace the progress so that travelers arrived at their destinations before snow fell in the mountains. Due to expert leadership, thousands of families successfully and safely navigated the Oregon Trail during one of the greatest migrations in human history.

For students, classroom learning is very much like traveling the Oregon Trail; it is a great mystery that they can't initially comprehend fully. Accomplished teachers, though, are like veteran trail guides since they know well the route to learning due to their experience. To empower students, teachers need to make learning as knowable as possible. Oregon Trail guides most likely described the route in general to the pioneers in their charge and then at the beginning of each day explained what they could expect in the terrain immediately ahead. Similarly, adept teachers give students the big picture of the unit ahead and then focus, lesson by lesson, on making the learning as knowable as possible.

The more knowable the learning path, the more students will be empowered to achieve excellence. The more learning is chunked into a step-by-step process, the more likely the chance of success. Found below are essential components that should be added to units and lessons.

BEGIN WITH THE END IN MIND

Big ideas drive the world. Likewise, units of study should arrive at an important destination: comprehension and application of some big, significant idea. For students to know the pathway ahead, they need to know the destination for their learning. "Begin with the end in mind" is a concept made popular as Habit Two in Stephen Covey's *The Seven Habits of Highly Effective People* (1990, 95–144).

Following this concept, Grant Wiggins and Jay McTighe in their book *Understanding by Design* (2005) advocate beginning any unit with this conceptual destination in mind. Units need to be guided by big ideas, called Enduring Understandings. The Enduring Understandings are meant to be knowledge or conceptual understanding that students can apply to their lives in the decades ahead. Actual student learning, though, is guided by Essential Questions, which frame the Enduring Understanding. The ability to answer the Essential Question at the end of the lesson or unit becomes evidence of accomplishing conceptual understanding of the Enduring Understanding (2005, 105–45).

A unit on the Oregon Trail might provide the following:

- Enduring Understanding: *Great rewards often require great risks.* Note that this is an example of an idea that students can apply to their actual lives currently and in the decades ahead. It is very much a core idea for study of what motivated pioneers to cross the Oregon Trail.
- Essential Question: *How do great risks lead to great rewards?* Note: Answering this essential question leads to comprehending the Enduring Understanding.

Sharing the essential questions for a lesson or a unit is the first step to making the pathway knowable for students. By knowing the big questions they need to answer, students' studies become focused. Teachers should regularly return to review the essential questions as they progress through a unit. To empower students, teachers need to make clear what relevant learning they will take away from learning.

MAKE VISIBLE THE STANDARDS FOR SUCCESS

Whether it is the Common Core for grades K–12 or college standards for a course, posting them and discussing them at the beginning of the lesson is a second essential step for students to "begin with the end in mind." Posting the standards (or placing them in an individualized learning plan) is essential for focusing students' thought process and giving them a target for their learning. Students become empowered when they know the outcome for their learning. For example, found below is a Common Core reading standard for grades 11 and 12. This would be for an activity on analyzing a writing selection:

• Analyze and evaluate the effectiveness of the structure an author uses in his or her exposition or argument, including whether the structure makes points clear, convincing, and engaging (Reading Standard 5).

For an eighth-grade math teacher, a Common Core standard for algebra reads as follows:

• Apply the Pythagorean Theorem to determine unknown side lengths in right triangles in real-world and mathematical problems in two and three dimensions (Algebra Standard 7).

By posting a standard or goal, there is no question about what is being expected in the upcoming activity. The standard should be explained so students thoroughly understand it. However, posted standards should be written, whenever possible, in student-friendly language. Therefore, these Common Core standards might be rewritten as follows:

• Analyze and evaluate the structure the author uses in the writing sample and explain how this structure makes points clear, convincing, and engaging.
• Use the Pythagorean Theorem to identify the missing dimension in a right triangle while solving problems.

As revised, the standards are much easier to read and understand. Teachers, though, may choose to go one step further and post the goals in the form of positive "I can" statements. For example, an English language arts teacher may post a more positive, student-friendly version of the Common Core reading standard:

- I can analyze and evaluate the effectiveness of the structure an author uses. I can look at the structure to see if it makes points clear, convincing, and engaging.

Along the same lines, a math instructor might post the following:

- I can use the Pythagorean Theorem to identify a missing dimension of a right-angle triangle while solving problems.

The challenge with writing goals or "I can statements" is to push them to a higher level of Bloom's Taxonomy. For example, a teacher may post "I can find the slope of a line given two points." This goal is totally verifiable and easily checked. It just lies lower in Bloom's Taxonomy—application—because it is the *use* of a skill. However, students can learn to calculate the slope of the line but not know what the slope means in terms of some real-world function.

A higher level of Bloom's Taxonomy—analysis—requires that students identify the *significance* of the slope in terms of an event, velocity or acceleration, for example. This would require the student to calculate the slope—the use of a skill—and interpret its meaning, a higher level of Bloom's Taxonomy. Note that this more rigorous activity incorporates both basic understanding and higher-level thinking functions.

Therefore, a more cognitively rigorous "I can" statement would be "I can interpret velocity using the slope of a line" or "I can interpret acceleration using the slope of a line."

This higher level of thinking is the place where businesses and institutions of higher education want students to function. "We are humans. We need to work at a level of something that a machine can't do," states Patrick Daisley, National Board–certified physics teacher. "If it is something that we can program an Excel spreadsheet to do—like finding the slope of the line—then that's not education."

Group goals for an activity will apply to all students, but what should a teacher do to individualize instruction? To really differentiate and individualize teaching, instructors can require either hardcopy portfolios (manila file folders work well) or electronic portfolios for students containing student work and individualized learning targets. Based on some form of diagnostic assessment at first, and then student work as it is completed, these individual goals allow a class to work on a variety of skills or concepts at one time. When one set of goals is achieved, another set is created. These portfolio goals allow each individual student to have his or her own personal direction for the course. Ideally, these goals should be created by the students and based on peer and teacher feedback. These individualized goals give the students direction about what they need to do to improve their skills or next growth steps if the original goal has been achieved.

To empower students, the expectations need to be made very clear. The first step is to identify clear goals and targets for the upcoming learning.

QUANTIFYING SUCCESS WITH RUBRICS

Once the standard (learning target) has been presented, the next step is to quantify success through the use of rubrics. A rubric is a list or a chart of descriptors that quantify different levels of success. The descriptors attempt to quantify the critical qualities found in successfully meeting the standard or learning target.

Rubrics, when used with models (explained below), provide tangible learning targets for students. By quantifying a target, students know what to aim for. A major reason students fall short in their performance is that they do not know what constitutes excellence. When teachers assess and assign scores using a rubric, the number given communicates what a score means based on tangible criteria. Through rubrics, teachers communicate to students where they excelled and where they fell short.

Rubrics can come in two forms: analytic and holistic. For many state-level assessments, students are evaluated using a holistic rubric, largely for expediency's sake. The holistic rubric gives descriptors for key traits, but all the descriptors for level 4, for example, are lumped together (see textbox 5.1). The entire test answer, assignment, or project is given only one holistic score.

While holistic rubrics remove some of the ambiguity of how scores are derived, the analytic rubric, which allows teachers to assess the quality of key individual traits, is a more precise tool at the classroom level to communicate to students where they stand on a variety of important skills. For example, in an informative/explanatory essay (see table 5.1), a student in writing may perform well in "topic development" and deserves a four and a three in "diction" but may underperform in "transitions" and receives a two for this category. Using a holistic rubric, the teacher or assessor, seeing that some parts of the writing are a four, a three, and a two, might assign a three to the writing project to average the differences. Using an analytic rubric, though, a score of four would be assigned to topic development while diction gets a three and transitions gets a two. From the student's perspective, he or she knows that extra energy needs to be directed toward diction and transitions. This level of communication provides precise feedback for classroom use.

TEXTBOX 5.1. COMMON CORE GRADE 9/10 INFORMATIVE/ EXPLANATORY WRITING HOLISTIC RUBRIC

CCSS.ELA-Literacy.W.9-10.2 Write informative/explanatory texts to examine and convey complex ideas, concepts, and information clearly and accurately through the effective selection, organization, and analysis of content evidence.

4—EXEMPLARY

- Skillfully introduces a topic. Includes a compelling hook, relevant background information, and a clear and focused thesis. Ideas flow smoothly from the hook to the thesis.
- Skillfully and logically organize complex ideas, concepts, and information so that each new element builds on that which precedes it to create a unified whole; writer skillfully and insightfully adds proper formatting (e.g., headings), graphics (e.g., figures, tables), and multimedia to aid comprehension.
- Develops the topic thoroughly by selecting the most significant and relevant facts, extended definitions, concrete details, quotations, or other information and examples appropriate to the audience's knowledge of the topic.
- Skillfully uses appropriate and varied transitions and syntax to link the major sections of the text, create cohesion, and clarify the relationships among complex ideas and concepts.
- Consistently uses precise and varied language, domain-specific vocabulary, and techniques such as metaphor, simile, and analogy to manage the complexity of the topic.
- Skillfully establishes and maintains an appropriate tone while attending to the norms and conventions of the format.
- Skillfully establishes and maintains an appropriate tone while attending to the norms and conventions of the format.
- Provides a compelling and thought-provoking concluding statement or section that follows from, supports, and extends the information or explanation presented.

3—PROFICIENT

- Sufficiently introduces a topic. Includes a hook, background information, and a thesis. Ideas flow from the hook to the thesis.
- Sufficiently organizes ideas, concepts, and information so that each new element builds on that which precedes it; writer adds proper formatting (e.g., headings), graphics (e.g., figures, tables), and multimedia to aid comprehension.
- Sufficiently develops the topic with facts, definitions, details, quotations, or other information and examples appropriate to the audience's knowledge of the topic.
- Sufficient use of transitions and syntax to link the major sections of the text, create cohesion, and clarify the relationships among complex ideas and concepts.
- Sufficiently uses precise language, domain-specific vocabulary, and may include some techniques such as metaphor, simile, and analogy to manage the complexity of the topic.
- Sufficiently establishes and maintains an appropriate tone while attending to the norms and conventions of the format. Lapses may be present.
- Provides a sufficient concluding statement or section that follows from and supports the information or explanation presented (e.g., articulating implications or the significance of the topic).

2—EMERGING

- While a topic may be introduced, a hook, background information, and/or thesis may not be adequately stated or developed.
- Ideas, concepts, and information are presented but may not build on that which precedes them; formatting (e.g., headings), graphics (e.g., figures, tables), and multimedia are inconsistent.
- Limited topic development. May include irrelevant or inadequate supporting details. May not be appropriate to the audience's knowledge of the topic.
- Transitions and syntax are inconsistent, predictable, or inappropriate. Transitions fail to create cohesion or clarify the relationships among complex ideas and concepts.
- Language may be imprecise or diction is predictable or repetitive; rarely includes techniques such as metaphor, simile, and analogy to manage the complexity of the topic
- Writing has limited style and tone; norms and conventions of the format may not be observed.

- Concluding statement or section is provided, though it may not follow from and/or support the information or explanation presented

1—RUDIMENTARY

- Some introduction exists, albeit it lacks a hook and/or a thesis
- Ideas are present, but little organizational pattern exists. Formatting (e.g., headings), graphics (e.g., figures, tables), and multimedia are largely absent.
- Some topic development is attempted but ineffective.
- Transitions may be attempted but are ineffective.
- Language is very imprecise and/or inappropriate.
- Writing lacks style and tone.
- An attempt is made, but it does not function to conclude the paper.

Internalizing rubrics becomes a key to student success, especially if teachers are working on lifelong skills like writing. For example, a four in Complex Ideas/Organization on a writing rubric may read, "Skillfully and logically organizes complex ideas, concepts, and information so that each new element builds on that which precedes it to create a unified whole." Whether the writer is a sophomore working to pass a state-mandated test for graduation, a reporter for a local newspaper, or an unhappy customer composing a letter to a restaurant owner, this standard for top score in Complex Ideas/Organization applies for many types of writing; its interpretation just changes due to the length and sophistication of the project. Carefully crafted rubrics, when studied, applied, and revisited again and again, create a permanent inner landscape in students that guides them when they are beyond the schoolhouse doors.

As with learning targets and "I can" statements, rubrics need to be designed, where appropriate, to measure higher levels of cognitive functioning.

Rubrics, for all their value, do have one shortcoming. Sometimes the use of a rubric implies that *only* that which is stated on the rubric is important and necessary for the task. In many instances, teachers cannot develop a rubric that includes everything that is important in a task, or the teacher may choose to assess only a few aspects of a task. If it is not on a rubric, does that mean students will not attend to it?

Write informative/explanatory texts to examine and convey complex ideas, concepts, and information clearly and accurately through the effective selection, organization, and analysis of content evidence.

	4—Exemplary	3—Proficient	2—Emerging	1—Rudimentary
Introduction *A. Introduce a topic*	Skillfully introduces a topic. Includes a compelling hook, relevant background information, and a clear and focused thesis. Ideas flow smoothly from the hook to the thesis.	Sufficiently introduces a topic. Includes a hook, background information, and a thesis. Ideas flow from the hook to the thesis.	While a topic may be introduced, a hook, background information, and/or thesis may not be adequately stated or developed.	Some introduction exists, albeit it lacks a hook and/or a thesis.
Complex Ideas/Organization *(A. continued)* *Organize complex ideas, concepts, and information to make important connections and distinctions; include formatting (e.g., headings), graphics (e.g., figures, tables), and multimedia when useful to aiding comprehension.*	Skillfully and logically organizes complex ideas, concepts, and information so that each new element builds on that which precedes it to create a unified whole; Writer skillfully and insightfully adds proper formatting (e.g., headings), graphics (e.g., figures, tables), and multimedia to aid comprehension.	Sufficiently organizes ideas, concepts, and information so that each new element builds on that which precedes it; Writer adds proper formatting (e.g., headings), graphics (e.g., figures, tables), and multimedia to aid comprehension.	Ideas, concepts, and information are presented but may not build on that which precedes them; Formatting (e.g., headings), graphics (e.g., figures, tables), and multimedia are inconsistent.	Ideas are present, but little organizational pattern exists. Formatting (e.g., headings), graphics (e.g., figures, tables), and multimedia are largely absent.

	4—Exemplary	3—Proficient	2—Emerging	1—Rudimentary
Topic Development *(B.) Develop the topic with well-chosen, relevant, and sufficient facts, extended definitions, concrete details, quotations, or other information and examples appropriate to the audience's knowledge of the topic.*	Develops the topic thoroughly by selecting the most significant and relevant facts, extended definitions, concrete details, quotations, or other information and examples appropriate to the audience's knowledge of the topic.	Sufficiently develops the topic with facts, definitions, details, quotations, or other information and examples appropriate to the audience's knowledge of the topic.	Limited topic development. May include irrelevant or inadequate supporting details. May not be appropriate to the audience's knowledge of the topic.	Some topic development is attempted but ineffective.
Transitions *(C.) Use appropriate and varied transitions to link the major sections of the text, create cohesion, and clarify the relationships among complex ideas and concepts*	Skillfully uses appropriate and varied transitions and syntax to link the major sections of the text, create cohesion, and clarify the relationships among complex ideas and concepts.	Sufficient use of transitions and syntax to link the major sections of the text, create cohesion, and clarify the relationships among complex ideas and concepts.	Transitions and syntax are inconsistent, predictable, or inappropriate. Transitions fail to create cohesion or clarify the relationships among complex ideas and concepts.	Transitions may be attempted but are ineffective.
Diction *(D.) Use precise language and domain-specific vocabulary to manage the complexity of the topic.*	Consistently uses precise and varied language, domain-specific vocabulary, and techniques such as metaphor, simile, and analogy to manage the complexity of the topic.	Sufficiently uses precise language, domain-specific vocabulary, and may include some techniques such as metaphor, simile, and analogy to manage the complexity of the topic.	Language may be imprecise or diction is predictable or repetitive, rarely includes techniques such as metaphor, simile, and analogy to manage the complexity of the topic	Language is very imprecise and/or inappropriate.

	4—Exemplary	3—Proficient	2—Emerging	1—Rudimentary
Style and Tone *(E.) Establish and maintain a formal style and objective tone while attending to the norms and conventions of the discipline in which they are writing.*	Skillfully establishes and maintains an appropriate tone while attending to the norms and conventions of the format.	Sufficiently establishes and maintains an appropriate tone while attending to the norms and conventions of the format. Lapses may be present.	Writing has limited style and tone; norms and conventions of the format may not be observed.	Writing lacks style and tone.
Conclusion *(F.) Provide a concluding statement or section that follows from and supports the information or explanation presented (e.g., articulating implications or the significance of the topic).*	Provides a compelling and thought-provoking concluding statement or section that follows from, supports, and extends the information or explanation presented (e.g., articulating implications or the significance of the topic).	Provides a sufficient concluding statement or section that follows from and supports the information or explanation presented (e.g., articulating implications or the significance of the topic).	Concluding statement or section is provided, though it may not follow from and / or support the information or explanation presented	An attempt is made, but it does not function to conclude the paper.

Source: "Common Core State Standards Initiative: Preparing American's Students for College and Career," 2012, accessed January 3, 2014, ttp://www.corestandards.org/ELA-Literacy,CCSS.ELA-Literacy. W.9-10.2.

An example of this is the use of the Grade 9/10 Informative/Explanatory Writing Rubric (table 5.1). For an essay, a social studies teacher may choose to use this rubric to assess and therefore direct the intent of a writing assignment. Does that mean, though, that grammar, skills covered in other Common Core standards but not being assessed with this assignment, do not apply? Certainly not. Commonly, teachers may assign major tasks but only assess a fragment of the total project.

When using a rubric for assessment, start by having students self-assess their own work before submitting it for teacher evaluation. Have students check the appropriate boxes and underline or highlight the descriptors that apply best to their work. This holds students accountable for understanding the contents of the rubric and checking their own progress against course standards. Students are also building that inner landscape essential to empowering excellence.

While rubrics are powerful tools for students, creating one collaboratively with a group of fellow teachers or as a department helps clarify the expectations for a common test, project, or assignment. Further, for schools implementing the Common Core, discussion of what each standard means and how its attributes should appear in student work goes a long way toward teachers understanding what is being expected by these widely adopted standards.

Rubrics are essential for communicating standards of success. The creation of rubrics demands that teachers identify precisely their expectations for student learning. And rubrics give students precise targets for academic success, empowering them to pursue excellence.

THE INQUIRY EXCEPTION

With inquiry, or discovery methods, sometimes students are supposed to discover the learning targets through the activity. In cases like this, it may be better to postpone presenting the learning targets, "I can" statements, and rubrics until that part of the lesson where it is appropriate to reveal them in order to not "spoil the end of the movie," if you will.

Nonetheless, these learning targets, "I can" statements, and rubrics will be directing the teachers as they present activities that direct student learning.

SUCCESS MADE VISIBLE: STUDY MODELS

Long before the advent of rubrics, effective instructors were using models and exemplars to guide students toward better performance. Examples of exemplary paragraphs, essays, lab reports, final projects, and so forth, are called models. Concrete models of successful work or projects can be that essential guide that leads to student growth. From persuasive speeches to volleyball serves, examples of excellence are essential when expecting students either to learn a new skill or to improve those they already have (albeit models are less helpful for conceptual understanding embedded in schematic understanding—science and math concepts, for example).

Models, though, unlike rubrics and essential questions, need not be presented at the beginning of the unit. Models are best analyzed as part of preparation for the activity they are meant to influence.

Of all the teaching strategies described in this chapter, models are perhaps the most significant since they are the manifestation of the learning target—something students can really grasp. By providing models and rubrics, and then thoroughly exploring how the rubric defines excellence in the model, teachers give students concrete examples of success.

Models for writing instruction, for example, can be particularly powerful. Writers trying to achieve a certain format do well studying exemplary models before the writing task begins. Take, for example, persuasive writing. If teachers want students to write proper persuasive essays, they need to show students examples of excellent writing products appropriate for their grade level. Models of exemplary work placed under document cameras work well for classroom discussions about a strong thesis, a well-constructed concession, and an effective call to action. As a class, teachers can lead the analysis about how the individual parts function to create a well-explained whole. In the margins, teachers can write notes as the students identify the essay's critical elements. Students can mark up their own copies.

Teachers can take analysis of models a step further by providing examples of high-, medium-, *and* low-quality work for skill development and deeper understanding. In this case, the teacher presents a project or assignment that has no score on the top. Using a rubric, students assess the quality of the project or assignment based on their understanding of the corresponding standards for success. Asking students to compare and contrast the traits of work samples of varied qualities requires them to deduce what a project or assignment of high quality is and what makes it fall short. Through their digging, they come to internalize the standards for success. Discussion about what constitutes excellence, what meets standard, and what may be missing from emerging work is a powerful way to imprint standards of success. When students know what different levels of success looks like, they have a target to aim for.

When completing complex technology projects, models can be essential for students to get all the elements correct. To create models that would serve as learning targets, teachers either create exemplars or collect them from past years. Either way, these models should contain all the elements required in the final product: the number of photos or videos required, appropriate background music, voiceovers, and text. Students review and analyze these examples. Therefore, before the students begin their projects, they know what the outcome of their efforts should be. These models inform students about the depth of content required for a quality project. Models provide students with the standards they need to meet when completing their projects—a vital component to establishing excellence in classrooms.

Models are powerful in career and technical classes as well. In art class, examples of past artistic efforts by former students can give current students an idea of what it means to meet standard, exceed standard, and approach standard. Examples of poor techniques and the mistakes that are produced are important learning tools. In a band class, students can listen to a professionally produced selection and then compare it against a recording of their own efforts. With a proper example of excellence, students don't become confused about the final sound and they work to discover what they can do to improve their individual efforts.

Of course, models are simply guides. Students should be given broad latitude to meet the desired outcomes in an individualized way. While some lessons can become disasters without models, damage can also be done when students think a model is a strict guideline. Never should models be used to stifle creativity or innovation—they should only be used to provide direction.

Models may be the single most potent strategy for moving students' skills to standards of excellence. Models need to be guides to point students in the right direction—but should not be a rigid formula. Analyzing the differences between excellent and average outcomes gives students the information they need to know to revise their own work. Students should be encouraged to exceed the model's standards whenever possible.

STUDYING ACADEMIC VOCABULARY FOR SUCCESS

One stumbling block for students is that they may know a concept but not know its academic name. When it comes to completing an activity, students stumble over the vocabulary required. Teachers would do well to make sure students understand completely the vocabulary being used, especially when the learning becomes technical. Terms like *hyperbole*, *allusion*, and *ambient* are not common in everyday conversation, for either adults or teenagers. Making sure that students know the vocabulary necessary for the work ahead is the first step in empowering them for success.

Not all academic vocabulary should be presented to students at the beginning of the lesson or activity in which they apply. Some words, like *acceleration*, for example, are loaded with misconceptions and lack of understanding. When the teacher uses these terms too early in the lesson, the students may already think they "know" this term and not attend to discussions and/or activities, failing to alter their preconceptions. In cases like this, the concept should be understood first and named later.

SCAFFOLD THE LEARNING PROCESS FOR SUCCESS

For meaningful learning to take place, teaching needs to be a thoughtful, intentional process for knowledge and skill building, one offering plenty of support to students.

When students are entering new, challenging cognitive domains, the challenge for teachers is how to move students forward. Models and rubrics are essential. They give concrete examples of the destination for student growth. But how do teachers go about actually boosting new skills themselves to a level that they meet and hopefully exceed course standards?

The key to student success is thoughtfully scaffolded lessons. Like the scaffolds used when constructing buildings, these organizers of thinking, analysis, and synthesis are crucial to the creation of a thoughtful, logical mental landscape that prepares students to perform complex tasks long after they have left classrooms. However, it is possible to make a lesson flow *too* step-by-step. Don't be overly prescriptive. Don't scaffold away the learning.

Like models of success, scaffolding is not meant to constrict student creativity. Scaffolds are designed to give students a model for thinking, knowing that teachers will allow flexibility if an effective, alternative process works better for the students. Scaffolds have limited use when creating conceptual understanding in areas like math and science, but for skill building and methodical thinking practices, they can be indispensable.

Sometimes, educators do a disservice to their students by assuming they have the thinking skills necessary to complete complex tasks of analysis, synthesis, or observation. Teachers should carefully structure the activity with appropriate scaffolding to make student thinking visible. Students who are falling short in the necessary skills can be pulled aside and helped in small groups. Scaffolding the learning process with careful structure and support material is a solid way to build thinking patterns.

The most common form of scaffolding is a graphic organizer. For years, English teachers have used simple T-charts to help students analyze the literature they were reading. In the left-hand column, the English students write a passage that would pique their interest, while in the right-hand column they would respond to the passage with some specific forms of literary analysis.

Venn diagrams, KWL charts (what you **K**now, what you **W**ant to know, and what you have **L**earned) and plot triangles, and a variety of graphics organizers are easily created on computers, saved as document templates, and ready for student use in electronic form or as a pencil-and-paper tasks, whichever is more appropriate at the time.

Scaffolds can also guide the investigative and conjecture process by teaching analysis strategies. Poetry and short stories can be analyzed by students in small groups using scaffolded analysis strategies. Two strategies,

TP-CASTT (pronounced *tip cast*) and SOAPSTones used by the College Board give students a series of steps in which they can dissect literature, analyze its components, and then synthesize an interpretation, the goal being to understand its meaning and significance. SOAPSTones—an acronym standing for **S**peaker, **O**ccasion, **A**udience, **P**urpose, **S**ubject, and **T**one—can be used to scaffold analysis skills for literary text. TP-CASTT Analysis— **T**itle, **P**araphrase, **C**onnotation, **A**ttitude, **S**hifts, **T**itle, and **T**heme—leads students from a surface analysis of the poem to its deeper meaning— theme—through carefully scripted prompts.

Cognitive strategies like TP-CASTT and SOAPSTones give students a regimented way to analyze and understand complex literature. With practice, though, these steps become so ingrained and personalized in students' minds that they can explore challenging selections and discover their meaning without giving thought to the steps it took to get there. These scripted activities direct students to explore and discover their own understanding of literature.

A form of scaffolding that is often overlooked is the checklist. A checklist of critical parts of the activity helps keep students on target as they create a final product or complete a lengthy project. Checklists come in a variety of forms:

- *Simple checklist*: This is a simple list of either the necessary components or a list of the required tasks. As simple as this may seem, checklists keep students on track. Checklists also result in fewer questions being asked of teachers and fewer omissions of critical elements when projects are complete. Further, checklists are a great way to organize activities in adult life.
- *Performance checklist*: These checklists are a great way to get students thinking about the quality of their work. Rather than a simple list of items to complete, a performance checklist instead asks students to rate the quality of their performance on a scale of one to four, one to five, or one to ten, with the highest scores being excellent quality. These checklists serve like a simplified rubric; they just lack the in-depth descriptors.
- *Templates*: These are the next step up from a checklist. A template prompts students to add specific elements to achieve a requested format. When students are learning to write a persuasive essay, for example, a template is a strong way to guide their learning. Reminders of what each element of the text should contain help students structure their writing. Again, scaffolds like these provide structure for students new to the process. As students become more proficient, they depart from the suggested organizational structure and write in a more individualized style. Microsoft Word has a powerful feature called "hidden text" that works well for templates. When students click on the Show/Hide button (it looks like a paragraph symbol in the tool bar), the template instructions disappear and the work looks like a regular draft.

- *Hidden slides in PowerPoint*: This concept is the same as hidden text except that rather than hide text, teachers hide the slides. These Power-Point slides are visible when students work on their projects but do not appear when the software is in presentation mode. Teachers using Power-Point as a student presentation tool can place instructions on hidden slides for the student slides that are to follow. Since PowerPoint is designed to be visual support for an oral presentation, hidden slides can be a very effective means of scaffolding critical speaking skills.

Graphic organizers model the thinking process; they make thinking visible so we can see where a student succeeds or falls short. Checklists model an organizational process. Templates and electronic templates model structures as well.

Scaffolding, as its metaphorical origin suggests, is a means of creating an inner landscape in students' minds. By transferring this knowledge to the students, teachers are empowering them for excellence.

KEEP LEARNING BITE SIZED—USE A WORKSHOP MODEL

One of the biggest mistakes teachers can make is to present too much material to students at a time. For an English teacher, it is easy to assign an essay at the beginning of the year and expect students to complete it and do it well. While this may work for high school advanced placement students, to most other students in other classes, breaking down the essay into separate writing assignments—intro paragraph, body paragraphs, and concluding paragraph, with mini lessons covering the characteristics of each—will lead to a better final outcome.

There is a saying that facilitators use when leading teachers through the mammoth National Board process: "You eat an elephant one bite at a time." The truth is that mentally, as well, students can consume only so much information or master so much of any skill in one setting. To empower students, they must feel confident. To help build confidence, build learning activities that progress in reasonable steps.

The reading and writing workshop model, advocated and fine-tuned by Lucy Calkins at Columbia University, starts with mini lessons not more than ten minutes in length. While the form of teaching below is explained in terms of the language arts classroom, the concepts can just as easily apply to math, science, or other academic settings.

The first step in the workshop lesson is to present a short mini lesson. To switch students into a "learning mode," they are asked to leave their desks and enter a "learning circle" in the front the classroom. Students leave their desks and either bring their chairs or come and sit on a carpet before the teacher with their writer's notebooks in hand. The instructor then presents an engaging "bite-sized" lesson on writing that zeros in on needs he or she sees in the student work.

Following the lesson, the students return to their desks and apply the lesson to their writing or reading. They work for twenty to thirty minutes diligently improving their prose. While students work, the teacher circulates among the students, answering questions and making suggestions to students on their writing—another bite-sized lesson in itself.

The final step is to share out. Students may volunteer. Often, the teacher has identified some selected examples of quality improvement; those students are asked to share their work.

The Lucy Calkins workshop method is an excellent illustration of taking learning, making it relevant, and then breaking it down into "bite-sized" chunks for students.

CONSTRUCT MEANING FOR SUCCESS

Whenever possible, turn learning over to students. The traditional classroom is very teacher centered, where instruction is dispensed in the form of worksheets and lectures. Student-centered teaching is the opposite of this. When students can learn best on their own, have them do so.

How might this look in an English classroom? Sooner or later, English teachers have to either teach or review the parts of speech. When teachers instruct grammar or writing improvement, eventually the parts of speech must come into usage. When talking about adding more description to writing, the use of the word *adjective*, for example, will inevitably be used. Students need to know the terms to understand any sort of discussion about improving sentence structure. But how is the best way to do this?

In a traditional classroom, the teacher would either give the students the definitions of parts of speech through lecture while the students take notes or have them copy them from a textbook. The next step would be to hand out a worksheet with a number of sentences and then direct the students to label the parts of speech found in them. Most of us can remember in our youth being drilled in the parts of speech using methods such as these. Worse, we remember diagraming sentences.

When empowering excellence, though, students are asked to construct their meaning on their own or in a collaborative setting. For example, rather than being given the definitions for parts of speech, students working collaboratively in groups would be directed to find them on their own. They would then identify the parts of speech assigned in sentences given to them. All this would take place in a workshop setting.

For example, a teacher would present to students the directions below. The instructions would be simple:

- Break into groups of four or five, with at least one person having a smartphone per group.
- Since grammar is so common on the Internet, I would like to have you find definitions for the following terms: *nouns, pronouns,* and *antecedents.* You may not use a textbook or a dictionary for this; you must find the definitions on your own using the Internet only.
- After you have found the definitions, identify the nouns, pronouns, and antecedents in the sample sentences.
- When you are finished, I will review your answers and place a plus over the answers that are correct and a zero over the answers that are incorrect. However, I will not tell you why the incorrect ones are wrong. You must figure that out as a group. You will keep returning to me to get them checked again and again until you get all your answers 100 percent correct.
- However, you may swap and compare your answers from group to group.
- Remember, the goal is to get your knowledge of this grammar 100 percent correct.
- When all groups are showing competence, we will follow with an individual check to see how each of you is doing in your own understanding.

This "discovery" method of teaching can be played in a myriad of ways in different content areas. The difference between this method of teaching and traditional methods is that the process lies with the students. Not only do the students learn the content, but also they learn how to *problem solve* and *find* the content, both of which carries over into their real lives. Plus, this builds students confidence and empowerment since they are the ones constructing their own meaning.

"Constructing Meaning" is the fourth principal in my book *Navigating the New Pedagogy: Six Principles that Transform Teaching.* You are invited to read that chapter and learn more about this concept in depth.

LET STUDENTS SUCCEED AT DISCUSSIONS

Whenever possible, let students lead the class discussions. As a group activity, Socratic seminars are a fishbowl strategy where students do the discussing among themselves based on questions the teacher has posed and the ideas and controversy students generate themselves. In a Socratic seminar, four to five students are seated in the middle of the class, with the remaining students circled around them. An additional seat—an open one—is placed in the middle as well. The students in the "hot seats" in the middle discuss the Socratic questions the teacher has created. The teacher observes and only redirects discussion if students get sidetracked.

Only those in the middle of the Socratic seminar may speak; those students circled around take notes on the discussion. If a student wants to make a comment or join the discussion, he or she must take the open seat in the middle. At that time, a single student may leave a "hot seat" and return to the outer circle. All students seated in the middle must participate before they can leave for the outer circle. A participation score can be given to students to assess speaking skills.

"Nun Thing" discussions are the next step in independent student discussion. Called the "Nun Thing" because the activity originated in a convent, this discussion format can be a tremendously powerful means of debriefing provocative reading or study. It was brought to mainstream use by the Teacher Leadership Project in Washington State and used near the conclusion of their multiday technology workshops as a tool for reflection. Again, a score can be given to assess participation.

The Nun Thing functions as a Socratic seminar, but the center-circle participants are limited to three in the hot seats with one left open. Again, only those in the center may participate. With the Nun Thing, though, Socratic-style questions are only used to prime discussion when it fades. Students are free to choose the topic or issue they desire. It just needs to relate to the study at hand. While the teacher may step in to stir discussion when needed, the Nun Thing is in a sense more student directed since students are the ones driving discussion from the beginning.

Once, I opened a Nun Thing discussion on the book *The Lord of the Flies* with my high school students. I did not offer a single topic, yet the topics discussed were as rich as if I were leading it. The Nun Things discussion format illustrates how competent students can be leading their own discussions when given the chance.

Whether teachers facilitate Socratic or Nun Thing discussion seminars, students are the ones who are exploring the topics and constructing their own meaning.

FREQUENTLY MONITOR PROGRESS FOR SUCCESS

Anyone who has spent time in the hospital has experienced nurses checking every few hours to monitor vitals. The doctors and nurses don't wait to the day of discharge to declare a patient healthy. They monitor the progress regularly and know precisely where a patient is on that journey toward recovery.

Should classrooms function any differently? Teachers should monitor progress through frequent informal assessment. The greatest thing that builds an internal pool of empowerment in the classroom is success; frustration and lack of success drain it. Frustration and struggle are not the same. With struggle, the frustration is still within check. With struggle, students continue to move ahead. By conquering their struggles, students build grit and pluck—something important for future success.

Frustration is that sense that nothing tried is working or the task is insurmountable. The student is filled with hopelessness regarding the task. To borrow a cliché, they want to "throw in the towel." Frequent informal assessment can help keep frustration in check. With intervention, frustration can be turned into struggle and a sense of the possible.

Informal assessment can be as simple as examining students' efforts for progress. If body language shows frustration, checking on the student is the simple first task. When possible, use probing questions to redirect a student toward the pathway to success. Show empathy and concern.

Collecting assignments for a quick check gives evidence of where students are on the road to meeting learning targets. Finding out where students are struggling and stumbling can create the basis for an activity addressing this when study resumes the next time.

Using handheld whiteboards in class is a great way to check for understanding in science, mathematics, and world language classes. Whiteboards are effective discussion aids since they hold thoughts and are good diagrammatic and graphical tools. During a "board meeting," each group has a whiteboard and is given a problem or a scenario to discuss and process together. When the groups are finished meeting, they hold up their whiteboards to be viewed by other groups and be questioned and commented upon. Teachers should refrain from entering these student-led discussions unless necessary. Since these boards are fluid and easily changeable, they can be revised as conceptual understanding changes. For the teacher, these are a solid means of assessing where students are in their formation of conceptual understanding.

Exit slips are an easy way to check progress. A few simple questions answered on a half-sheet of paper and left with the teacher can be a quick form of accountability for the student and informal assessment for the instructor. A sentence like "Name three important concepts you learned about the periodic table today" gives the teacher an idea of what the student is taking away from a lesson.

This gathering information from a variety of sources is sometimes referred to as "student voice" since it reveals how well students are progressing and allows the teacher to make strategic changes in instruction, if needed.

Frequent and varied assessment gives teachers valuable information about how a class is progressing individually and as a group.

* * *

While on the Oregon Trail, pioneers traveled a journey that lasted months and covered almost two thousand miles. In many ways, the educational journey through a school year is a two-thousand-mile journey itself. The key to making that journey a success is first to know the destination—through enduring understandings, standards, rubrics, and models—and then to make the process knowable—through scaffolding—and break the journey down into bite-sized chunks, with frequent assessments to see how students are progressing. The efforts to build success step-by-step are essential to giving students the tools and understanding for empowering excellence.

Shift 6

Grade by Mining Student Data

Mrs. Westerman keeps a running total in her grade book. All grades are averaged. All assignments count toward the final grade. She believes this keeps students on their toes at all times. A strong work ethic pays off. Amy has averaged Cs on her summative assessments. Due to accumulating points for all her homework, though, she is receiving an A− for the semester.

Matt, though, has missed numerous daily assignments and submitted his first big essay two days late, resulting in the grade of B for the paper dropping to a D—he was penalized one grade for every day it was late. As a result, he received a D for the first quarter.

Mrs. Westerman's unit on the American Revolution, though, really interested him, and his scores for that unit are much improved. It's near the end of the semester, now. Matt is confident he could pull an A on the final project for the unit, but due to his missteps early in the first quarter, the best he could get for the semester is a C+. Should he reach for this level of excellence when there is no reward for his efforts?

Still, Matt is in better shape than many other students. Due to a few missing assignments, a handful of his friends, mostly pretty smart kids, have opted to not complete the final project at all since at best they could not significantly bring up their grades due to all scores being averaged in.

Many teachers with decades of experience recognize Mrs. Westerman's classroom practices since it was the way many—including myself—once taught (and many still do). Academics were central to our grading method: important summative assessments and important activities received higher points. Subtly lurking below grading practices, though, was an emphasis on rewarding students for conforming to expectations and showing a good work ethic. There was also an underlying belief that students should be rewarded for their daily work with points, much like employers would reward an employee with pay: the more challenging the assignment, the more points were rendered. Full points were rewarded if the assignment was complete or done properly. Partial points were given if the work was not complete. Points represented payment, the system went. This method of grading, many felt, was building a strong work ethic and preparing students for the real world of work. These were largely effort grades.

The problem with many traditional teaching and grading practices is that rather than *encouraging* excellence, they subtly strong-armed students, spurring them to perform through a system of reward and punishment. Summative assessments scored on rubrics have very much an academic focus in Mrs. Westerman's class, but averaging scores works against those who have lower scores to start the term. Further, adding copious amounts of homework points—with the possibility of extra credit too—resulted in semester grades skewed higher or lower than the students' actual level of skills and conceptual understanding.

Many experienced educators knew well the flaws in the system; they just blamed the student level of effort. When grades did not match their academic skill level, students were labeled "overachievers" who padded their scores with homework or extra-credit points. Capable students who were late with their assignments or chose not to do them at all were dubbed "underachievers."

Traditional teaching and grading practices have the potential to cloud academic proficiencies and mask deficiencies. For those who have trouble playing the game sufficiently, grading became punitive and discouraging.

To create a more optimistic, academically focused classroom environment requires a shift in thinking. The purpose of this chapter is to offer teachers and professors an alternative, a road map for *working with* students. It's a move away from punitive grading practices toward a focus on building academic skills and conceptual understanding, and awarding grades on the growth that occurs.

SHIFT IN THINKING: MINE STUDENT DATA FOR GROWTH— DON'T AVERAGE SCORES

Math teacher Patrick Smith uses a traditional one-hundred-point grading scale for scoring his daily take-home math assessments. In order to track student progress in this skill, he keeps all scores for the eighth-grade Common Core Math Standard "Prove polynomial identities and use them to describe numerical relationships" (HSA-APR.C.4) clustered together in his electronic grade book. He does this to assess individual student growth in his classroom. Amir's scores for "polynomial identities" take-home assessments appear in figure 6.1.

Mr. Smith is pleased by the growth he has seen in Amir's ability to understand and apply the concept of polynomial identities. The thing he needs to calculate is what grade he ought to award for this set of scores. Looking at the scores, it would appear that Amir started in the high sixties in proficiency range (typically the D+ on a one-hundred-point system) for the first assessment. Low scores were common for the first efforts, Smith remembers, since this was the first time introducing this concept. Common problems appeared for many students. As a result, the second round of assessments was better. Amir continued to apply Smith's feedback to this. As a result, his final scores for this concept were in the mideighties (the mid-B range). At question, though, is what grade should Smith award Amir for this set of scores?

In a traditional grading system where all scores may be averaged, the zero would be factored in. The average score for this set of numbers would be 63 percent, resulting in a D grade in the traditional percentage-based system. But does 63 percent really pinpoint the student's actual ability to understand this concept? Without the zero, the student's average score would be 78 percent, a closer assessment of the student's actual abilities by the end of the term, which is in the high eighties. The question needs to be asked, though: should the lower scores be factored in at all if the student has risen to a higher level of skill or conceptual understanding later in the term?

To answer this question, let's view this set of numbers a bit differently. Let's switch from academics to sports. Take a look at the chart a second time, viewing the numbers as the yardage gained by a high school football running back over the first five games of his senior season. This time, rather than a teacher, a college football recruiter is looking at the numbers to assess running skills. The zero this time represents a game missed due to a violation of team rules. The remaining numbers are statistics for yards run per game. Looking at the numbers, would a football coach scouting players for his college team view this running back as capable of running sixty-three yards per game (the average) or as a young man showing the potential to run close to ninety yards a game as the season progresses? Certainly the zero as a team violation would be a concern (as its equivalent, a missing assignment, is a concern), but a team violation is a disciplinary issue—not something that would be factored into the player's capacity to run.

| 67 | 75 | 0 | 87 | 86 | Grade? |

Figure 6.1. Amir's scores for "polynomial identities" take-home assessments

In short, a coach scouting for a college team would look at this running back as someone who has the potential to rack up to close to ninety yards per game. This is the most accurate assessment of the young man's running skills at the time. It also is based on the running back's strengths and not his deficits. Shouldn't teachers think about grading students differently?

A major shift in student assessment philosophy is that not every score should count when assigning a final grade—in short, no more averaging. This means a shift away from weighting every score to mining student data for evidence of the levels of skills and conceptual understanding at the end of the term—and then basing a grade as closely as possible on the highest point of student growth and achievement.

These two concepts align closely with grading experts. According to Thomas Guskey and Jane M. Bailey in *Developing Grading and Reporting Systems for Student Learning*, "If grades are to represent students' current level of achievement or performance, we must ensure that they are based on evidence of what students can do now and not what they were able do last week or last month" (2001, 47). Further, Rick Wormeli in *Fair Isn't Always Equal* writes, "A grade represents a clear and accurate indicator of what a student knows and is able to do" (2006, 103). Ken O'Connor in *How to Grade for Learning* agrees: "For knowledge or skills that are in any way cumulative or repetitive, teachers need to look particularly at the more recent information to determine grades" (2002, 127).

Needless to say, this method of grading contrasts greatly from the old system of penciling in column after column of scores in a paper grade book and then punching out a final average on a calculator when the semester or trimester concludes (or doing the equivalent in an electronic grade program). With this new method, the teacher looks at selected scores and uses professional judgment to determine a grade.

What teachers are doing is mining student data to assess an accurate score. No mine would produce high-quality silver if all the ore were mixed into the refining process. By its nature, the refining process is a procedure where the unnecessary is discarded so a pure element can be extracted. Assigning grades should work this same way.

Like mineral refining, teachers mine student data for evidence of skill levels and conceptual understanding. In this process, not all scores are used to create a final grade. Early or outlier scores are disregarded as students show a level of proficiency in their understanding and skills.

Teachers need to look for reliable data. "The quality of evidence considered is important, as well. Any single source of evidence on student learning can be flawed or misinterpreted," states Guskey (2001, 48).

Look at the pros and cons of traditional grade assignment versus this contemporary means of assigning grades. Traditionally, one of the reasons for counting all scores into a grade has been that if all scores do not count, students might not try their hardest on assignments early in the grading term. Students may loaf about early in the quarter or semester and wait until the end to get to work if there is not some sort of penalty for not working early. (In the reality of the classroom, this can happen with students regardless of how a teacher grades.) Basically, averaging scores is viewed as a lever to prod students toward progress. By starting the punishment early, teachers show students they mean business since all grades count. Students who squander their early chances in the beginning of the term will pay for it later on. At first look, this seems logical until you look at the alternate side of the argument: giving early scores the same weight as later scores can also discourage later attempts to improve. Students might say, Why should I try since I got a D on the first assignments, and since I'm getting Bs now, the best I can get is a C for the course anyway?

Another reason some give to count all scores is to create a sense of accountability. For the highly motivated student, low scores do in fact inflict punishment, much like a speeding ticket stings the conscientious driver. Typically, motivated students will do what the course requires. They want a good GPA; therefore, they want good scores. To them, every score matters. Grades work as levers to pressure these students forward.

Yet experience shows that zeros and low scores do far more harm than good in the long run in motivating most students. For the barely motivated student, poor grades can be very discouraging. At the whiff of failure, these students back down and retreat. As Wormeli writes, "A surprise to some: Low grades push students further from our cause, they don't motivate students. Recording a D on a student's paper won't light a fire under that student to buckle down and study harder. It actually distances the student further from us and the curriculum, requiring us to build an emotional bridge to bring him or her back to the same level of investment prior to receiving the grade" (2006, 103).

Guskey agrees that low grades, while they may be unavoidable, do more harm than good: "No studies support the use of low grades or marks as punishments. Instead of prompting greater effort, low grades more often cause students to withdraw from learning" (2001, 34–35).

In fact, depending upon how they are assessed, these poor grades, while they may reflect a student's lack of enthusiasm for a class, may not correspond to their measureable knowledge or ability.

Finally, there is the question about how perfect we expect our students to be. An occasional lapse may simply reflect a person's humanity. On occasion, everyone "drops the ball" in some part of his or her life. We are, after all, human. Should a lapse at an inopportune time devastate a student's grade for a course? Those teachers who are member of the "school of high accountability" would say so, but in reality, even high performers stumble. Grading systems need to take the occasional lapse into account. There needs to be a certain element of forgiveness for an occasional lapse in assignments, papers, and projects. "It is not uncommon, for example," Guskey writes, "for some unusual occurrence in a student's life to impinge on his or her performance on that particular day and adversely affect assessment results" (2001, 48).

These times of challenge for students present opportunities for teachers. "Students thrive because teachers bend a little here and there to teach in ways in which students can best learn and so remain hopeful about their prospects," Wormeli observes (2006, 92).

The challenge for teachers comes in overlooking zeros to assess the skills and understanding that exists. This concept of every assignment or test counting for a grade is very ingrained in educators, and moving away from this requires a shift in thinking. Old habits die hard, until the teacher experiences the academic growth that can happen when students are freed from the occasional misstep. Again, this new vision of assessment empowers teachers to sift through student scores to assign a grade based on clear and convincing evidence of skill levels and understandings the student has achieved by the time the term ends.

So, how should zeros or missing work be viewed? The best answer is that a zero in a grade book is simply a mark of a lack of evidence. Rather than a zero, a teacher can as easily put an M in the grade book to represent missing work or an I for incomplete. For that assignment, there was simply no data to mine to assess a student's skill level or conceptual understanding.

Giving students multiple opportunities to achieve a standard, providing them with chances for abundant formative feedback (from the teacher as well as peer and student self-assessing), and then assigning a grade based on the growth that takes place is a critical component of *Empowering Excellence*.

The great benefit of mining student scores for the best scores is the optimism it builds in students. When better scores are factored into the grade and the lesser scores and occasional missteps overlooked in grade calculations, students have an incentive to grow. Where students start in the learning process becomes far less important and less discouraging than where they finally arrive when they themselves have the power to bear down and study and wipe out the past. Early poor performance is not viewed as permanent or pervasive—which would support a pessimist explanatory style. Early scores are viewed as temporary, fixable, and something a student can strive to improve with the effort being rewarded. Optimism powers better performance.

Finally, this system of measurement makes sense. If a farmer were asked about his corn crop, he would not assess the final output by the cold spring he had or the slow growth experienced by June. He would celebrate the warm July and August days that delivered to him head-high stalks and a bumper crop of ears. The growth and final outcome is celebrated.

Implicit in this concept of grading is the idea that students will be given numerous opportunities to improve themselves for each standard or skillset. They will also receive plentiful feedback (which we will discuss more in depth later) in order to grow in their skills and conceptual understanding.

To mine student data, student scores need to be clustered around a standard or skill set in the grade book. To accomplish this requires a grade book organized to gather data around each standard attempted (O'Connor 2007, 53–60). These attempts are recorded so that students and teachers can see evidence of growth (or lack thereof). The scores are merely the evidence the teacher will use for assessment. The final grade for those set of scores is assigned by the teacher based on his or her professional judgment.

After scanning the student scores, the instructor tries to assess where the student is in his or her growth at the end of the grading period. The teacher endeavors to mine this data for clear and convincing evidence of the highest level of student understanding or skills for that category—which is what students are really capable of doing. These grades for each standard are in separate columns and impact the course grade. See Mr. Smith's calculations for polynomial identities in figure 6.2.

To mine student data efficiently, scores need to be clustered around a standard (Common Core in K–12) or skill set. If a hard-copy grade book is used, teachers merely scan the clustered scores and assign an average of two highest scores, to honor growth. An electronic spreadsheet can also be designed to create these functions to speed calculations, although the grade book should have an override feature to allow professional judgment the final say.

Rather than simply adding points in the grade book for the assignment being completed, the teacher assesses it for the standard being practiced (knowing that not all activities needs to be assessed, of course). This allows formative work, if recorded in the grade book, to inform the teacher about how well the student is progressing toward the standard. These scores can also inform the final assessed grade for a standard or skill set.

Name	Polynomial Identities Assessment 1	Polynomial Identities Assessment 2	Polynomial Identities Assessment 3	Polynomial Identities Assessment 4	Polynomial Identities Assessment 5	Summative Grade for Polynomial Identities
Amir	67	75	0	87	86	*86.5*
Raven	72	75	81	79	80	*80.5*
Justin	79	83	84	0	84	*84*

Figure 6.2. Mr. Smith's grade calculations for polynomial identities

One thing educators need to wrestle with, though, is what constitutes clear and convincing evidence. Will two scores suffice, or are multiple scores necessary to assess the level of skill or conceptual understanding? What if a student displays abundant evidence of understanding in classroom activities but fails to produce enough scores posted to the grade book? What if the formative assessments look solid but the student, under pressure or feeling stress from some problem in his or her life, fails the summative assessment?

Again, this is where professional judgment should override the electronic spreadsheet. While some may say this will result in "fuzzy" math, weighing all scores equally can skew grades unfairly if the purpose of grading is to honor the growth in skills and conceptual understanding.

When teachers mine student scores to accurately assess a student's skills and conceptual understanding at the term's end, grades actually mean something because they are an accurate reflection of the level the student has grown to by the end of the term. This method encourages excellence because it builds hope and honors the hard work students put into their studies.

Shift 7

Assess Work Ethic Separately

Mrs. Westerman is a very demanding teacher, her students say. In particular, she is very confident in the effectiveness of her no-late-homework policy. If daily assignments are not completed and turned in on time, students get zeros in the grade book. For major projects like essays, students' scores are reduced one letter grade for each day they are late. A handful of capable students are failing her classes since the zeros and reduced scores populating her grade book are dragging down their percentage grade for the class.

Work ethic is critical for success in life, Westerman tells herself. *I would rather have students fail now and learn to work than fail later and lose jobs when they have families to feed.*

Late work. Missing work. Assignments not completed due to absences. For all the wonderful things about the teaching profession, what to do when students are chronic in not completing their assigned tasks is a challenge. A good work ethic is critical to success in life. Yet, how can excellence be empowered when students are negligent in completing their assigned, relevant practice work?

For all the benefits of standards-based grading, the problem of what to do with students who do not complete assignments is still a conundrum. It would be nice to report that the Common Core and standards-based grading usher in a new era of achievement, where *all* students are motivated to complete their work due to clear learning targets, opportunities to improve, and eliminating averaging in favor of assigning grades based upon growth. While movement toward this assessment style is a step ahead in the evolution of effective educational practice, there will still be students who turn in incomplete work, forget assignments, or simply choose not to do them.

Some of this can be attributed to the student's place on the continuum toward adult maturity. Learning to be responsible and meet deadlines are skills that need to be learned for success in life, no matter the grade level. Some late or missing work can be explained by lack of interest in a class. Some can be explained by students not knowing how to do the task or skills required of the assignment. Some can be blamed on family problems, issues with their peers, or busy schedules due to activities and after-school jobs. Regardless of the grading philosophy a teacher follows, late and missing assignments is the reality of working with youth—and even with adults.

While occasional zeros or late work can be overlooked due to missteps, regular missing assignments should cause real concern. Regular missing work can be the sign of a discouraged student, but it also may reflect a lack of discipline, an absence of interest in the course, or a conflict in priorities. Missing assignments can be a sign that a student struggles in the class.

In many classes, missing work here and there will not impact student academic progress. Some missing assignments, though, can be of such importance in terms of growth that not completing them is very detrimental to academic growth. In courses like math, for instance, missing assignments that are key to sequential growth in conceptual understanding can stunt student progress, perhaps impacting understanding for the rest of the course (and even the courses that follow). Each assignment may be of great value. This level of work should not be missed, and teachers need to develop strategies to deal with it. What avenues exist? Is there a better way to handle this than handing out zero after zero?

Let's look back to the way missing work was often handled in a traditional grading system. In a traditional classroom, grades were often used as a lever to motivate students to learn. For some students, though, it was more than a lever; it became a stick used to whip irresponsible behavior. If a teacher tells students that assignments need to be completed by a certain date or they receive a zero (or a lower letter grade for each day it is late), that educator is communicating to students that work habits are being assessed at a higher value than measurable academic achievement. The zeros for late work are averaged in, thus dragging down the students' grades and, possibly, their GPAs. The students' grades suffer, but more drastically, their conceptual understanding or skills suffer too since they were ultimately not held accountable for the work—which may have a major impact on their academic future.

Make no argument. Work ethic is a key element to making steady academic progress. It certainly needs to be addressed, and it will be further on. The question remains, though, did penalizing or not accepting late work truly help students build a stronger work ethic in the long run? For the grade-conscious student, having scores snipped by missing work can certainly jolt them into responsible action. But just as often, this penalizing of students by reducing the value of work due to late submission—or not accepting it at all—can be more discouraging than beneficial.

"Our traditional ways of using assessment to motivate students to want to keep trying—the rewards and punishment of grades—often don't work as we hope they will," writes Rick Stiggins (2007, 38). Is there a better way to build work ethic and responsibility?

Understanding by Design trainer and national Association for Supervision and Curriculum Development (ASCD) presenter Erik Powell tells the story of how his mentor, Gary Finer, addressed this problem. When Powell, early in his career, approached him regarding handling missing work, Finer, an exceptional teacher made wise by decades of classroom experience, said this: "If students don't turn in their work, and I give them a zero, I simply let them off the hook. I don't want to do that. I want them to get the work in. I want to hold them accountable for what needs to be done." Rather than doling out zeros for late or missing work, Finer simply demanded that it be done, late or not.

Thus, handing out zeros for missing assignments is not effective. "We believe that students should learn to accept responsibility and should be held accountable for their work," Thomas Guskey writes. "Nevertheless, we know of no evidence that shows assigning a zero helps teach students these lessons" (2001, 144).

Requiring that key assignments and assessments be completed, even if late, while possibly looking soft from a traditional grading perspective, really demands more accountability from the student. The message is one not of punishment but of concern: This assignment is important to your growth as a student. It must be done for that reason. A second message is just as powerful and relevant to life: if you are assigned a task, it needs to be completed.

Isn't demanding that students get the job done—even if late—a greater form of accountability than simply giving them zeros? Isn't it better for students' academic growth?

A cornerstone of empowering excellence is that work ethic—academic preparation—is a skill that needs to be taught. Like scaffolding or models mentioned in shift 5, students need to understand what being a fully responsible individual feels like. Holding them responsible for getting all work done—even if some is turned in late—is a valuable first step in creating that functionality.

A second problem with a traditional method is that the grade book, when it becomes populated with scores reduced for late submission, does not communicate academic progress to teachers, students, or parents. It becomes useless as a diagnostic tool to assess where students have problems. Some grades are entered at full value because they are received on time. Others have been knocked down in value since they were not received when due. If the grade book is to become a tool to which teachers and students refer to track academic growth, shouldn't the information be as pure as possible?

The answer is to enter all student work in a grade book at its assessed score (against a standard) no matter when it is turned in. This way the scores can communicate academic progress to teachers and students. Knocking a final score down two letter grades because it was late a couple of days does not clearly communicate where students are in their academic achievement (O'Connor 2007, 19). These scores represent false, confusing data. Having a policy of placing zeros in the grade book—when a student may show proficiency in a skill or concept but the assignment was not accepted because it is late—skews the data further.

If educators believe that a grade book's primary purpose is a means of accurately recording academic progress, giving reduced scores or zeros runs contrary to intent (unless, of course, work is not received despite repeated attempts from the teacher; at this point, the zero, or an "M" for missing, communicates no data for the skill or conceptual understanding).

The question arises, though, of what to do when students—despite interventions—have zeros (or Ms for missing) for a skill or concept. Let's go back to the list of Amir's math scores for "polynomial identities" assessments that were used in the previous chapter (see figure 7.1).

When looking at this set of scores, there are really two skills represented. One skill is the ability to work with polynomial identities. The scores in figure 7.1 represent a growing ability with this skill. By the end of the term, Amir has grown in his skills to receive scores in the 86–87 range, which reflect abilities at the end of the term. If the math teacher, Patrick Smith, believes that grades ought to be an assessment of summative growth—much like a farmer would judge the success of his crop by the final height of his corn—then Amir would receive an 86.5 for this particular skill.

The second, not so readily apparent skill is academic preparation. Out of five math assessments, Amir completed four. If Mr. Smith "mines student data" to assign a grade for these scores, Amir's skill level at the end of the term would be assessed at an 86.5, which translates into a B or B+ in a traditional grading scale. If a teacher uses the traditional method of averaging all scores—and leaves the zeros in as punishment for work not completed—the grade for polynomial identities becomes a 63 percent or a D. The question remains, Is this D really an accurate assessment of the student's skill

| 67 | 75 | 0 | 87 | 86 | Grade? |

Figure 7.1. Amir's scores for "polynomial identities" take-home assessments

level in this math concept? No. The 86.5 is a closer measurement of the student's capability.

The presence of the zero is troubling since assessments were a major part of the course and the student completed four of five assignments or 80 percent of the assigned tasks for this concept. Nonetheless, the teacher has adequate data upon which to assess the student's skill level.

What if there were more zeros? Again, can the teacher, using professional judgment, assess a grade for the set of scores? If so, the teacher mines student data and assigns a reasonable grade that reflects the growth for that student.

What if no assessments were turned in? If all scores for assessment were zeros due to missing work, then the teacher lacks the clear and convincing evidence necessary to assign a grade for that skill set. For that skill set, the student receives a zero, and that will impact his grade quite negatively. The difference, though, is that the grade was not assigned as punishment for incomplete work. The teacher simply lacks evidence to assign a score, and when the student completes enough work to produce such evidence, a grade can be given. Until that time, no evidence exists, and a grade will suffer.

The challenge comes when the teacher has some but not enough conclusive evidence to assign a grade for a set of scores. Look at this set in figure 7.2.

Mining data becomes more challenging since only one score exists. For teachers in real-world classrooms, this represents the challenge they occasionally face regarding disengaged students. Having little data puts teachers in a quandary since assessment experts recommend using multiple sources of information (Guskey 2001, 48).

Here is a solution. If the single polynomial-identity assessment represents an *authentic* skill level, then the teacher should assign a score of 82 for this math skill. Although the polynomial-identities skill level has been assessed as an 82, the student's work habits will still be assessed. The student will still be held accountable for her work ethic or, in this case, the lack thereof. How to hold students accountable will be discussed later in the chapter.

BE PROACTIVE ABOUT TIMELINESS

The best way to deal with zeros or late work is to prevent them to begin with. By doing this, teachers can also help students build lifelong skills of timeliness and organization. Here are a few practical tips:

0	0	0	82	0	Grade?

Figure 7.2. Scores for another student's work in polynomial identities.

- Make assignments as engaging and relevant as possible. When students see the value of schoolwork, most dig in and get it done. If it is an enjoyable assignment as well, you can almost guarantee a high completion rate.
- Collaboratively decide with the class on major assignment deadlines whenever possible. Everyone likes a say in decision making. For major assignments, propose a deadline and see if it is reasonable. If students desire more time, flex to their wishes, but state that timeliness is part of the bargain. Students may have major assignments due in other classes at the same time. By flexing, teachers improve their chances of student timeliness.
- Teach students to be organized. Any teacher who has taught long enough will witness students with reminders written on the backs of their hands. It brings a chuckle, but writing assignments on the hand really isn't effective productive behavior. Students need a formal means of organization, and teachers need to allow time for this organization and to actually oversee that it takes place. Daily planners, electronic tablets, and cell phones are a great way to record assignments. Teachers should also have some blank monthly calendars on stock for students who don't have a planner but prefer hard-copy organization. Model and post the same deadlines in a visible way in the classroom. Have class assignments and deadlines available on a website easily accessible for students and parents.
- Recognize students' busy schedules. Students, like adults, have lives outside of school. Many have after-school jobs, athletics, activities, and commitments to religious and civic institutions. Some just want to hang out with their friends, skateboarding, playing video games, or social networking. Teachers need to be conscious about intruding upon this time for homework assignments. Most students will allow some time for homework, but a big assignment dumped on them that is due the next day is not fair—and can be a source of plenty of zeros. If an assignment is due the next day, give reasonable time in class to complete it first, or allow them a few minutes the next day at the opening of class to finish it up.
- Check in the assignments as soon as possible by placing a plus sign on a roster. Meet with students who are missing work immediately (either that day or the next) to address why the assignment has gone missing; establish a deadline then for when it will be completed. Let students know that a parent contact will be made if that deadline is missed.
- Use the power of technology. Cell phones are ubiquitous. When students are missing work, keep them after class or ask them to come by after school. Have them call their parents or guardians right at your desk. When they are through, confirm the problem with the parents and talk about solutions that can take place.

- Many electronic grade books have e-mail features. Create a generic message in a word-processing program and then copy and paste it into e-mails to parents; customize as needed. Using a template like this saves time.
- Continue to press the importance of timeliness in assignments; for students who continue to be untimely or delinquent in their homework, continue with follow-up calls at home. Refer them to their counselors for a parent-student meeting if work continues to be incomplete.

MAKE ACADEMIC PREPARATION A COURSE STANDARD

Work ethic should not be overlooked by any means. Make it a standard for the course. Remember, the Common Core, while quite comprehensive, need not be the only standards assessed. Work ethic should be assessed as well. Having a place to account for missing or partially completed assignments or assessments in the grade book and report card is critical since work ethic is an important component to success as a student and as an adult. Parents and guardians, too, want to know the effort their students are putting into their studies.

One answer to missing or late work is to assess work ethic as a separate standard for a class, sometimes called personal responsibility or academic preparation (henceforth referred to as academic preparation). Having a separate score for "academic preparation" allows this important category to be addressed while keeping assignments and test scores based on standards a pure reflection of students' capabilities. The academic work itself retains the same assessment value whenever it is received. However, the academic-preparation score becomes a standard recorded in the grade book; it is based on the student's overall work ethic. A strong, consistent work ethic is represented with a good academic-preparation score. Consistent late work impacts the academic-preparation score negatively. For students who are very responsible, a good score in this category communicates this reward.

While an academic-preparation score is a departure from traditional grading practices where academic skills and work habits were rolled into one grade (a concept called "grade pollution" by Stiggins), this separation makes sense. Work habits or work ethic is different than the ability to display academic skills or conceptual understanding. By making these different and separate scores, teachers will then have the data to work with students to improve each. A student who knows the material but doesn't get the work in is very different from someone who would like to complete the work but does not have the skills or understanding to finish the task. By separating them in the grade book, teachers have the data to attack each and chart progress as students improve.

To accomplish this, teachers need to create a reasonable window in which assignments are accepted. If work is received on the assignment deadline, the student receives the score in the grade book. This acknowledges the work was completed on time. If the deadline is missed, the student receives an L if it comes in late (along with the numeric score for the assignment at its full academic value) or an M for missing if it doesn't arrive at all.

Having a separate score for academic preparation allows this important category to be addressed while keeping scores based on standards a pure reflection of students' academic capabilities. When teachers try to trouble-shoot why academic progress is stalled, these marks provide the data necessary to find out if the issues are a matter of skills and conceptual understanding or a lack of discipline. Dealing with a student who struggles while submitting all his work requires a different tactic than one who struggles but turns in little work.

In order to get the most work completed, classroom assignments must be designed to propel students ahead toward meeting standards for the class. Students need to see the work's value. No busy work is acceptable in this model of teaching. This schoolwork is very much like sports practice on the playing field. Like purposeful sports drills, class work and homework must be worthwhile activities that advance student skills and build conceptual understanding. While some activities may be more valuable than others, each should be a building block to achieving success in a standard. Missing work handicaps students, since this work is vital to achieving academic success. Low skills or understanding and missing work can be a sign of a struggling student, one lacking enthusiasm for the course, or both. Nonetheless, these students need attention.

Since all schoolwork is considered relevant by the instructor, the teacher adds scores in the grade book as a means of assessing progress and awarding a final score for that standard. Remember, though, that not all class work needs to be turned in and recorded. Students should be afforded plenty of opportunity for penalty-free practice. Opportunities where teachers stroll the classroom, informally assessing student practice work and giving feedback, should be abundant.

Where this academic-preparation score is reported is a matter of philosophy. An academic-preparation score can be one of the standards a teacher assesses that become part of the grade itself. If academic preparation is to be factored into the actual course grade, the score can make up 10 percent of the final grade (Wormeli 2006, 106). In either case, the academic-preparation component should never impact a student more than one letter grade on the semester report card.

A second school of thought advocated by some grading experts is to report academic preparation separately in the form of a report-card comment. This is common in elementary schools. Secondary teachers who have used this method, though, have found that if homework isn't calculated somehow into the grade, students frequently do not do it. This led these teachers to adding an academic-preparation standard that was calculated as part of the grade *and* was made a comment on the report card.

By recording academic preparation as a separate standard with limited impact, the course grade remains largely a purely academic score. It is recorded separately as a standard since it is viewed as a measure not of academic prowess but of personal discipline. If students desire better grades, they have to focus on improving skills and conception understanding—and they can do this by improving their work ethic (which results in a higher score for the academic-preparation standard too). Essentially, student work ethic becomes seen as the vehicle for academic excellence. It becomes its own separate standard due to its importance.

One big advantage of having a separate academic-preparation standard is the information it gives parents or guardians. Rather than being rolled into the scores for assignments and activities (such as a lower score for late work), academic preparation stands alone and becomes an indicator to why a student may or may not be progressing academically in a class.

To assign a score, educators need to identify what constitutes different levels of academic preparation. This requires the teacher to scan assignments and assessments for missing and/or late work and then to assess to what degree a certain amount of work "meets standard" (Proficient) for on-time completion and at what point the performance "exceeds standard" (Exemplary). Next comes the cut for what is "emerging" and what is "rudimentary" in the course. The teacher then assigns a score for this standard accordingly.

In an algebra II class, for example, a teacher may reason that completing seventeen out of twenty assignments on time (note: work is still accepted late) "meets standard" (Proficient) and nineteen and above "exceeds standard" (Exemplary). "Emerging" may start at twelve out of twenty assignments completed punctually, while eleven and below is considered "rudimentary."

Differentiating this new academic-preparation standard for students is appropriate as well. For example, a student starts a grading period and regularly misses work. The teacher sets up an intervention: a conference with the parents, for example. Due to this intervention, the student improves his or her work habits to a point where no assignments are late or missing. This student may very well be worthy of an "exemplary" score if the remaining assignments for the term meet class deadlines.

When teachers set a deadline for schoolwork, they also need to set a reasonable window in which late work will be accepted. Most teachers are buried under paperwork that needs to be assessed. Accepting September's work in December would create an organizational nightmare. One reasonable solution is to accept the work while the learning is still relevant to class time.

Say, for example, students need to complete an analysis of the key ideas and themes of the novel *To Kill a Mockingbird* (ELA Grade 9–10 Key Ideas and Details Standard 2). Accepting that work while the class is working to meet the standards assigned for *Mockingbird* makes sense. Students have until that unit is over to get the work completed. When they move on to the *Romeo and Juliet* unit, the *Mockingbird* standards are no longer accepted. Those not completed receive an M for missing in the grade book, which may translate into a zero for grade calculations since the student displayed no level of proficiency in that standard. Having no data for a student due to missing work is far different than a zero for that activity because the assignment was submitted late and the teacher refuses to accept it. However, the teacher may allow the student to meet standard by finding details to meet Key Ideas and Details Standard 2 in *Romeo and Juliet.*

If the students submit no work for a standard, this may be highly detrimental to their final grade for the course. What is needed is balance and fairness when accepting late work—for both students and teachers. Educators do not need to become victims to students' busy lives or poor decisions. They just need to be fair.

Of all the concepts in this book, making academic preparation a separate standard or skill (while keeping the academic score unchanged) is one of the hardest ideas for veteran teachers to accept. Their grade books have been the places where they can *discipline* students who choose to be late with their work or show ambivalence toward their courses. By either reducing grades for late assignments or refusing to accept them at all, these teachers are sending a venomous "to heck with you" message to the students who seem to be transmitting that same message themselves to the teacher and or the course they are taking.

Great teachers, though, rise above a personal fray when dealing with their students. Ron Prosser, a wise and respected Spokane school counselor and college professor, said, "Never get into a power struggle with teenagers, because teens always win. They win the battle but may lose the war." Prosser understood how students will dig in their heels when a conflict de-evolves into a power struggle. While these students may win the power struggle, they may end up doing themselves great harm in terms of academic progress. The wise educator thus avoids these power struggles.

In the end, avoiding the power struggle with students over the completion of assignments is at the core of separating scores for academic progress from scores for academic preparation. By having a separate score for academic preparation incorporated into a grade book, students *are* held accountable. Those who work diligently see their efforts assessed with a high score. Those who falter in getting their assignments completed—for whatever reason— receive lower scores. These scores, though, become the basis for discussion about what responsible academic preparation looks like and how a student can work to accomplish that. They can become a measurement of how students are growing in their ability to get work completed on time.

Academic scores based on the Common Core (or college standards for courses), though, should remain a pure measure of what a student knows and is capable of doing at the end of the term. If academic preparation is factored into that final grade, it should never have an impact of more than one letter grade. A term grade should, to as great a degree as possible, reflect the growth in academic skills and conceptual understanding.

As Carol Ann Tomlinson and Jay McTighe state in *Integrating Differentiated Instruction and Understanding by Design*, "A grade should give as clear a measure as possible of the best a student can do" (2006, 133).

BUILDING RESILIENCE

Holding students' toes to the fire, as the saying goes, helps build resilience, commonly called "grit." Rather than allow a student to dismiss completing assignments, the philosophy of having teachers persistently require that *all worthwhile work* be completed has the potential to build resilience in students.

In his book *Fostering Grit*, Thomas R. Hoerr states, "A focus on success in life means that, beyond teaching the three R's, we must also teach character, emotional intelligence, responsibility, and an appreciation for the complexity of human diversity. We must also teach the virtues of *grit*—tenacity, perseverance, and the ability to never give up" (2013, 1).

Hoerr cites a 2013 report from the U.S. Department of Education titled *Promoting Grit, Tenacity, and Perseverance: Critical Factors for Success in the 21st Century* that expresses concern for students who are learning to "do school but are not developing the life skills to persevere in the face of challenges they will face in the real world." The report notes that "educators, administrators, policymakers, technology designers, parents and researchers should consider how to give priority to grit, tenacity, and perseverance in curriculum" (Hoerr 2013, 3).

Certainly, one motivation for teachers assigning worthwhile, rigorous homework and activities is to promote "grit, tenacity, and perseverance in curriculum." Completing rigorous activities in a timely fashion certainly builds personal skills that are a necessity for success in the work world. The schoolhouse then comes to reflect the reality of the everyday work world where all tasks assigned are expected to be completed if one hopes to stay employed. Schools can become an important instrument in teaching this lifelong skill as long as they require that any activity be completed in a timely fashion.

How is the best way to build resilience? Certainly one very effective way is to assess work ethic as a separate standard that impacts the course grade. By making this important skill something to be assessed—something worthy of significant formative instruction—teachers work to build "grit, tenacity, and perseverance in curriculum."

When work ethic is assessed separately, grades are no longer used as a means to promote or punish—they are simply measurements, much like a farmer taking a tape measure to his corn to see how high the stalks have grown. By separating academic *progress* from academic *preparation*, teachers are able to differentiate their efforts when assisting students with the critical lifelong skill of "work ethic."

Efforts at academic preparation are essential for empowering excellence. By making these important skills a separate standard, teachers can measure them. Teachers can work with students to improve these most important skills. By making academic-preparation skills a separate standard, teachers can give them the attention they deserve, thereby helping empower students to pursue excellence.

Shift 8

Communicate Progress Clearly

Students in Mrs. Westerman's class have become accustomed to receiving a variety of scores on assignments and assessments. Simple daily work is worth five points, where a more complicated activity can be valued at fifteen points. Final unit tests may be worth up to two hundred points to balance out the homework points that students accrue. Mrs. Westerman's weekly essay tests are worth twenty points each. Major essays are scored on the Six Traits of Writing and are worth 150 points. Students often need to use calculators to figure out their grades for activities.

For many school-age children or young adults, one of the greater mysteries of the world is how grades are calculated. How separate scores are churned into what eventually becomes a possibly life-changing GPA is mysterious for most students—and a big part of their lives. Look back on college courses. How many times did grades received make absolutely perfect sense? Grading practices differed greatly from instructor to instructor. Assessment practices varied widely. Teachers and professors were like judges passing rulings, and there was no higher court to turn to if the final grade seemed unfair.

Teacher and professors themselves are the source of this mystery. While some may enjoy the "power" that directing students' futures gives them, many educators find grading uncomfortable. Present to students grades that are lower than expected, and their students' faces fall. Poor grades can cool the positive relationships instructors have with their students. Rightly or wrongly, students take grades personally.

Great teachers and professors are typically nurturing people, and delivering painful grades runs contrary to what they perceive to be their professional mission, much like delivering a negative diagnosis is a challenging part of being a physician. Education is a business that thrives on positive relationships. Determining that final unsatisfying grade can be an unsavory task when scores point in that direction. Assessment just has to be done, though.

So far, this book has discussed ways of creating supportive work environments, means of assigning grades, and methods of dealing with missing work. The next step is to make all scores available to students and educate them fully on how grades are derived. This is the antithesis of the old-school grade book penciled with scores, locked away in the teacher's top desk drawer. Since academics are keys to students' futures, shouldn't this mystery be revealed to them if educators are going to ask them to take full responsibility for their lives and the choices they make?

The next step in empowering excellence is to make the grading calculations as transparent as possible. If teachers are to empower excellence, students need to know how their scores impact a final grade and what they can do to influence that final outcome.

MAKING SCORES MAKE SENSE

No student benefits from mystery grading. When students work hard completing assignments and studying for tests, they expect good outcomes as a result. Less than anticipated grades can be discouraging. To borrow a cliché, it takes the wind out of their young sails.

If teachers want to empower students to grow in their skills and conceptual understanding, these young students need to know what their scores are and what they can do to improve them. This means making the academic-assessment process as transparent as possible. This leaves no room for mystery in grading. Students need to know that they will be assessed on their best efforts—their height of optimal growth, as was explained in the concept of "mining student data." This averaging of the highest scores, with an emphasis placed on the latter score, is something students should be able to roughly calculate for themselves.

For students and teachers to trace their growth, scores need to be organized around a standard or a skill set. By doing this, students can view the growth they are experiencing in a particular area of study. They can look at the standards and skills where they are doing well and direct their attention to areas where they need to grow to get their desired grades. To accomplish this, students need access to their scores in the form of organized data.

How should a teacher organize a grade book? First, look at the way a traditional grade book is organized (see figure 8.1). The assignments listed in figure 8.1 are a mixture of writing and literature assignments. Scores for assignments vary depending upon the length and complexity of the assignment. In fact, this view comes from my grade book before my move to standards-based grading.

If teachers were to make scores configured in such a fashion available to their students, the only numbers that make immediate sense are the grades in the form of a percentage in the last column. The traditional purpose of a grade book is to store scores and tally them for a final grade. Making sense of the other scores requires some rough math calculations to see how the students are doing on separate assignments (e.g., Jane Doe's score of thirty-four out of forty points for the Making Predictions Paragraph shows a grade in the traditional B range, and John Smith's twenty-six out of forty points looks to be a D grade when using the traditional percentage cut scores).

In this grade book, scoring is inconsistent. Nor are scores organized around skills or standards. As is quite obvious, the scattering of a variety of scores in a grade book prevents it from being an easy-to-understand tool to assess student progress in different skills or content areas.

Adopting a four-point scale that aligns to the rubrics and scoring standards immediately improves understandability. Keeping standards (or skill sets if they represent bundled standards) grouped together provides immediate feedback to how a student is progressing in class.

As Ken O'Connor states in *How to Grade for Learning*, "The most appropriate way to organize a grading plan would be to base it on individual standards or benchmarks" (2002, 51). Note how, in this format (see figure

	Does Life Imitate Art? (8 pts.)	What Are People Implying? (10 pts.)	Intro to Paragraph Writing (10 pts.)	Setting for Your Life (15 pts.)	Conflicts in Your Life (10 pts.)	Looking for Theme (12 pts.)	Where is the Narrator? (10 pts.)	Making Predictions Paragraph (40 pts.)	Foreshadowing in Interlopers (38 pts.)	Irony in the Interlopers (5 pts.)	Percentage/Total Possible Points: 158 Grade
Jane Doe	1	10	10	15	6	12	10	34	32	4	84.8% B
John Smith	6	8	7	12	10	8	8	26	30	3	74.6% C

Figure 8.1. Traditional grade book. Scores above are organized around activities themselves. The higher point value represents an assignment with more questions or activities involved or possibly more complexity: the more work required the higher point value. The "Making Predictions Paragraph" score was based on a scoring rubric.

8.2), standards are lumped together, but a final column is included for semester assessment where the teacher assigns a final grade for this set of standards based on the growth that took place over the grading term.

The understandability of the grade book is improved greatly by organizing it around standards and moving to a 4-point grading system—which is tied to rubrics. If a 2 means approaching standard, 3 means meeting standard, and a 3.5 to 4 means exceeding them, then teachers and students can immediately calculate how students are progressing against the expectations for the course. Further, if John Smith wants to boost his semester grade to a B, it is clear that work in standard RL.11.6 might give him such a bump.

If the purpose of the grade book is to communicate where students are in their academic growth and areas where they need to grow, organizing scores around standards makes sense. Organized in such a fashion, the grade becomes more than a means of capturing and crunching student scores. It becomes a dashboard whereby teachers keep organized measurements on a

	RL.11.1 Explicit Meaning/Inference in "I Hear America Singing" (Unweighted)	RL.11.1 Explicit Meaning/Inference in "I, Too, Sing America" (Unweighted)	RL.11.1 Explicit Meaning/Inference in *A Raisin in the Sun* (Unweighted)	RL.11.1 Explicit Meaning/Inference in "Mammon and Archer" (Unweighted)	**RL.11.1 Explicit Meaning/Inference Semester Assessment—Weighted**	RL.11.6 Grasping Point of View in "Let's Hear it for Cheerleaders" (Unweighted)	RL.11.6 Grasping Point of View in "How to Poison the Earth" (Unweighted)	RL.11.6 Grasping Point of View in "Advice to Youth" (Unweighted)	**RL.11.6 Grasping Point of View Semester Assessment—Weighted**	Academic Preparation—10 percent of grade	**Tabulation of Scores/Grade**
Jane Doe	3.25	3.5	3.75	3.75	**3.75**	2.75	3	3.5	**3.25**	4	**3.6 A-**
John Smith	3	0	3	3.25	**3.15**	2.75	3	3	**3**	3	**3.04 C+**

Figure 8.2. Language arts categories. Scores above are tabulated on a 4-point scale and organized around standards. Notice how a glance at these scores, organized around standards, can quickly communicate student progress. The teacher is "mining student data" to derive a summative score for a standard. For that reason, "data" scores are unweighted in the grade book, while the summative score are weighted and impact the final grade for the term. Note the column for Academic Preparation and how the 0 for one missing assignment for John Smith was factored into an academic-preparation and the final grade. *Source:* Derived from the "Common Core State Standards Initiative: Preparing American's Students for College and Career," 2012, accessed January 3, 2014, http://www.corestandards.org/ELA-Literacy.

variety of skills and concepts, just like the speedometer and gauges keep track of different functions of an automobile. If students have online access to an electronic grade book, then they can check their academic progress as needed from a computer or smartphone.

Whether or not teachers have access to an electronic grade book, they can still make students masters of their own destiny by distributing to them individual progress charts organized by standards. When students receive back their assessed assignments or tests, they can pencil in their scores on their student progress charts. This allows them to see where they are academically in terms of a standard, how they have grown, and where they need to apply their energies to improve a grade. Taking a few minutes to write in scores during class provides the students with the opportunity to ask the questions they need regarding their progress.

Again, the point of organizing grades around standards is to allow students to know precisely where they are academically. They can also take satisfaction in their growth displayed as their scores improve. By witnessing their own growth, students are empowered to advance toward excellence

MAKING GRADES MAKE SENSE

An urban legend tells of a wife who always cut the end off of a ham before she placed it in the oven to bake. One day, her husband asked her why, and she responded that she sliced the end off because that was always the way her mother traditionally prepared a ham. At a later date, the husband approached his mother-in-law to inquire about this unusual practice. His mother-in-law responded that she always sliced the ham to make it fit—her oven was a small one.

There is no question that many practices in education are passed down and repeated only because that is the way they are traditionally done. Certainly, aspects of grading practices fit this definition. The use of a one-hundred-point scale is one of them. For many veteran educators, its use is well-ingrained.

In the one-hundred-point grading scale, the scores a student earns for the grading term are added up. The total points the student accrued is divided by the number of points possible. As a result, a percentage is calculated, and a grade, with some variation, is determined largely as follows in traditional grading:

90–100 percent = A or Excellent
80–89 percent = B or Good
70–79 percent = C or Satisfactory
60–69 percent = D or Poor
59 percent and lower = F or Unacceptable (Guskey and Bailey 2001, 68)

How and from where these percentages evolved remains a mystery, but the thinking is so entrenched in education that, at the time of this writing, electronic grade programs use this scale as a default setting. Why should 90 percent be the bottom line for an A? What is so significant about 70 percent that it is the starting point for competence?

This book, for the most part, aims to challenge many assumptions about assessment and grading. The traditional one-hundred-point grading system is no exception. While its origins are unknown, the percentage system makes some sense from a completion-oriented philosophy of education (as opposed to a standards-based philosophy). Students need to gather a majority of points in a course to receive any credit for it (60 percent). Competence starts at 70 percent of completion. Excellence represents achieving 90 percent of points possible. Summative assessments typically receive greater points than daily work and smaller tasks, but all points are eventually stirred together and students' grades are decided based on the percentage of points possible in a grading term. With this system, consistent completion of daily work—which typically constitutes a high percentage of points possible for the term—can skew a grade upward, while a lack of daily work can often result in a D or an F, regardless of how well students score on important summative assessments.

The percentage system plays out reasonably well in real life. Take golf, for example. People who complete 70 percent of their shots with good form and accuracy are most likely competent golfers (as long as the remaining 30 percent are reasonably on target). Likewise, being on the green in regulation 90 percent of the time would represent excellent golf skills.

The challenge in shifting from the old percentage system to a four-point system is recalculating grades. No longer would a teacher say, You have 90 percent of points possible. Congratulations, you have an A. Instead, the teacher would say, The average summative score of all your standards is a 3.60. Congratulations, you have an A.

Essentially, a percentage system was designed to work on converting a variety of points offered for test and assignments into a letter grade. Four-point scales are common in standards-based grading systems since this aligns with the rubrics used for scoring and GPA calculations. The grades that signify competence in the one-hundred-point system represent the top 30 percent of the points possible (a grade of C or above). In the four-point system, competence or better inhabits the top 25 percent of "points" possible (a three or better). Simply put, the systems don't precisely mix. One of the great challenges for veteran educators is unhitching themselves from the old grading percentages and allowing them, like an unmoored boat, to drift off and disappear.

In the best of all standards-based worlds, letter grades would be dropped and grades would be represented in the one through four method on the report card. In reality, though, states and institutions of higher learning require letter grades as a final mark for a term. Even at the collegiate level, where a course grade may be often given on a four-point scale, the grade is converted into a letter format. For example, when a student receives a 2.5 at the University of Washington, it is viewed as a B−. Simply, letter grades are part of our thinking and part of our system for now. That said, the one-hundred-point grading mentality need not be.

Regardless of philosophy, percentages need to be assigned at some point because electronic grade books are nothing more than glorified spreadsheets. As in the old system, these percentages determine the cut-off point for what becomes an A, B, C, D, and F. (Note: Some educators advocate for A, B, C, and F but no D, based on the mentality that students either should meet proficient—a C—or better or they should not pass a course at all.) These new percentages, though, need to be based on a new well-communicated philosophy and not on old tradition. Based on classroom experience, for example, keeping a B at 80 percent of the possible points may place the entry point for "above average" work too high when using a four-point system. The same may go for starting As at a simple 90 percent.

Grade cut-off points need to thoughtfully arrive at since basically a four-point scale (four, three, two, and one) is being converted to a five-point scale (A, B, C, D, and F). The way to do this is to tie the basic definitions for grades back to the descriptors found in rubrics.

Four-Point Scale Descriptors Found on Rubrics

4 = Exemplary
3 = Proficient
2 = Emerging
1 = Rudimentary

Corresponding Descriptors for Letter Grades

A = Exemplary
B = Very Proficient
C = Basic Proficiency
D = Approaching Proficiency
F = Emerging, Incomplete for Class

When converting the four-point system to a letter grade, teachers and administrators need to ponder, *What should a letter grade look like in terms of four-point descriptors?* In other words, the final grade needs to make sense in terms of the rubrics used to create it. For example, *What should an A look like?* is a good place to start. The immediate answer may be that an A should have scores of all fours. While it may be true that an A+ would contain all fours, if all fours were needed to get any kind of an A, very few students would achieve this unreasonable standard for academic excellence.

A reasonable definition for an A− might be that the student has more fours that threes in the grade book. This would mean that as a starting point, over half the scores in the grade book are Exemplary and the remainder are Proficient. Out of ten hypothetical scores, an A− might look as follows:

A− = 3, 4, 4, 3, 3, 4, 4, 3, 4, 4 (four 3s and six 4s)

The average score—the mean—for the above numbers would be a 3.6. This would result in a grading scale of 3.6 to 4 for an A grade for a term. This, interestingly, translates into 90 percent.

Similarly, the base line for a B− would be to place that score one step above where a C+ would be. If that is the case, the next question is, what kind of scores should constitute proficiency? It seems reasonable to suggest that for students to be proficient in a course, they would need to be receiving mostly threes for the work they are completing. To step onto the bottom rungs of a B or Very Proficient, the student would need to receive at least one four (one score above standard) to cross the entry point and enter the Very Proficient realm.

In a hypothetical set of ten scores, a grade of B− might look as follows:

B− = 3, 3, 3, 3, 3, 3, 3, 4, 3, 3 (all 3s, one 4)

The average score—or mean—for this set of numbers is a 3.1. That would result in the grading scale of a 3.1 to 3.59 for a B grade. The 3.1 translates into 77.5 percent for a B−. Out of a set of ten scores, that would mean that a B− would start with one four, while a B+ would have at least five fours. This makes the grade range for a B 77.5 to 89.9 percent. Again, it is the philosophical distribution of threes and fours that determines the grade cutoffs, not some traditional percentage system.

What should the grade of a C look like? If a C is to mean "Basic Proficiency," then the majority of scores ought to be threes. Then what should a C− be? Again, if a C is a mixture of twos and threes, then the student should have more threes (Proficient) than twos (Emerging) if he or she is to receive a grade that reflects Basic Proficiency. Again, look at another set of numbers. In a hypothetical set of ten scores, the grade of C− might look as follows:

C− = 3, 2, 3, 3, 2, 3, 3, 2, 3, 2 (four 2s, six 3s)

The entry point for Basic Proficiency would mean that the majority of scores would be Proficient for a C−. The C− would start at 2.6 or 65 percent on the electronic spreadsheet. The range of a C would be 2.6 to 3.09, or 65 to 77.49 percent.

What constitutes a D is really determined by what should be considered minimal proficiency to graduate to the next level. For some educators, straight twos might be the minimum to pass a student along. But is that fair to the student? Certainly a number of threes should be in the mix. A grade of D− might look as follows:

D− = 2, 2, 2, 2, 3, 2, 2, 3, 2, 2 (eight 2s, two 3s)

With these scores, the philosophical minimal performance for getting credit for a class is 2.3 or 55 percent. A minimal proficiency range of somewhere between 50 percent and 60 percent is typical. Again, the question is how the chosen percentage aligns with a hypothetical set of rubric-based scores.

In summary, a very workable percentage system that aligns to a four-point scoring system goes as follows:

Descriptors for Letter Grades

A = Exemplary: 3.6–4.0 (90–100 percent)
B = Very Proficient: 3.1–3.59 percent (77.5–89.9 percent)
C = Basic Proficiency: 2.6–3.09 percent (65–77.49 percent)
D = Approaching Proficiency: 2.3–2.59 (55–64.9 percent)
F = Emerging, Incomplete for Class: 2.29 and below (54.9 percent and below)

Note: We arrive at the need for percentages since most electronic grade books are spreadsheets and require percentages to calculate grades.

These are only grading suggestions. Teachers, schools, and school districts can tweak these suggestions as they see fit.

By tying grading percentages to a hypothetical set of rubric-based scores, educators unhitch themselves from antiquated tradition and tie themselves to a solid grading philosophy about what excellence looks like. The above grading percentages are very workable suggestions. Again teachers, schools, and school districts need to collaborate to determine how grades will philosophically be derived from the rubrics and scoring that represent the standards for the courses.

PROVIDING PLENTIFUL OPPORTUNITIES TO GROW

If teachers are to empower students with a desire for excellence, students must have a sense that they can control their own academic futures. To create this sense of optimism, students need to be offered numerous opportunities to grow in a standard or skill set. This growth, though, is not accidental but teacher planned. As is mentioned in shift 11, plentiful feedback is the compost in which academic growth will thrive.

Through this process of numerous opportunities to grow, teachers are assessing growth, placing scores in the grade book, and preparing to "mine student data" to assign a grade that reflects the highest points of student accomplishment. This concept of "mining student data" with multiple scores blurs the rigid wall that traditionally separates formative from summative assessments.

Assessment expert Rick Stiggins advocates plenty of penalty-free practice before student work is assigned scores. This practice without grades being assigned is designed to free students to make the mistakes they need to learn and grow. Formative feedback is applied liberally during these practice times (see shift 11), with all work leading to summative assessments, which will impact the student's grade. The only problem with this method is that sometimes summative assessments—for whatever reason—do not always capture students at their best. Some students, for example, may suffer from performance anxiety. Family life and personal problems may intrude upon performance. Other times, students may make one small but critical mistake in their thinking during their summative assessment that negates the good work they completed during practice sessions.

The solution is to base grades not on one snapshot taken during one summative assessment. The answer lies in taking multiple samplings of progress along the way and to use the scores that best reflect the students' skills and conceptual understanding to determine the grade. These multiple snapshots could all be summative assessments, but they could as easily be a mixture of summative and reliable formative work. In other words, rather than having students work toward one great day of measurement, the teachers are taking measurements along the way to determine where students are in their growth. They are regularly gathering reliable student data to use to calculate the most accurate final grade for their students that they can.

In the end, teachers collect a variety of scores around each standard or skill set—both formative and summative. Typically, these scores, nourished by plentiful feedback, will improve as the term progresses. In the end, teachers apply their professional judgment when viewing these scores and assign a grade that reflects the high point of growth for students.

UNDERSTANDING THE SHIFT IN THE PATTERNS OF GRADING

Switching to a standards-based grading system often has one unintended consequence that teachers and schools need to prepare for: grades early in the term may often be lower than what students experienced when scores were calculated using traditional practices. This switch from a completion-of-work-based grading system to a standards-based model for assessment requires that students and their parents/guardians reorient their expectations for grades early in the term.

The traditional method of doling out large numbers of points for work completed heavily favored the compliant student with the strong work ethic; extra-credit points for completing additional assignments (or picking up points for worthy public service like canned-food drives or attending content-related extracurricular activities) skewed the grading system further. Teachers created the term "high achiever" for the students who went into overdrive to get As in a course when their skill levels were actually much lower.

Standards-based grading requires a completely different allocation of points. It focuses on the "wheat" of academic achievement and scatters the "chaff" of daily work points and extra credit. Rather that tying the point level to the complexity of the project or the effort it took to complete (multiparagraph essays receive 150 points in the grade book, for example, while daily work receives 10 points), each grade in the standards-based environment is an assessment of skill level or conceptual understanding. Therefore, the "high achiever," whose actual measurement of academic achievement barely meets the new standards, may see lower grades than he or she experienced in previous courses, at least at the outset. Note, though, that the superior work ethic, when properly focused, will boost grades as the term progresses.

On the other hand, students who occasionally missed an assignment here and there but had very solid academic skills may see higher grades than they earned in the past. Since new grading methods focus on measuring what students know and are able to do, this group of students may do better gradewise.

When teachers begin grading against standards fixed for a grading term (a semester, for example), students may start the term with lower grades than what they have experienced before with traditional grading methods. For schools that send out first-quarter and mid-quarter reports, the change in grades can startle parents. The same applies for families who have real-time online access to electronic grade books. For many students, initial grades start lower than they are used to. "Students who receive a mark of 1 or 2 on a 4-point grading scale during the first or second marking period of the school year are making adequate progress and are on track for grade level," Thomas Guskey writes. "To parents, however, a report card filled with 1's and 2's, when the highest mark is a 4, is cause for real concern" (Guskey and Baily 2001, 85).

When one thinks about the standards a student should achieve over the progression of a course, this all makes sense. If the assessment criteria are appropriately normed for the course, many students *will not be competent* in their first attempt to meet a standard for an activity or task. In fact, if most *did* meet competency on their first attempt, the standards for "meeting standard" for that course may be inappropriately low. On a four-point scale, for example, a student may receive a 2 for his or her first attempt at completing a task or showing conceptual understanding. This is to be expected, especially if the teacher is using the activity as a diagnostic assessment. With practice and knowledge-building, proper teaching strategies, and plenty of descriptive formative feedback, the student score for that standard should rise to a 3 or a 4 over the course of the grading period. As a result, the students' overall grades improve as they become more proficient in the skills and conceptual understanding required for the course. In other words, grades rise as the term progresses and students become more proficient in content knowledge and skills.

Found in figure 8.3 are actual high school class scores for informative/explanatory essay-writing skills assessed early in the school year (stripes) and two months and two papers later in the term (in gray). These scores were based on the performance of three sophomore honors English classes and scored against Common Core 9–10 grade standards for informational/explanatory text: WHST.9-10.2. Since expository writing was not new to this group of students, the teacher used the "Power of Myth" assignment as a diagnostic assessment at the beginning of the year. The high school teacher's projected outcome was to build informative/explanatory essay-writing skills to a level expected for that grade level by the time they arrived at Springboard Unit 2, Embedded Assessment #1 a few months later. In this graph, the majority of students received Cs or below on the diagnostic essay. One-quarter received Bs; there were no As. After plentiful feedback on their first two essays, the majority of students received Bs and twelve received As on the Springboard assessment, the third essay. Only one student received a grade lower than a C.

Figure 8.3 illustrates the outcome of this profound change in grading philosophy and teaching practice. Notice how nearly all the students received Cs or better by around the middle of the term. This was the growth goal for students.

Under the traditional grading methods, teachers operate within the paradigm of the "bell curve," which contrasts greatly with the final outcome charted in figure 8.3. When teachers talk about "curving" test scores, they are attempting to create a bell curve for grading in their classrooms. That teachers or professors would do this make sense. In many instances, a "bell curve" statistical model mirrors reality. When charting data (take longevity, for example), there is often a congregation of outcomes, which create the top of the bell curve, and outliers. What holds true in many facets of real life, then, must hold true for education, too. Under this bell-curve statistical model, most students would get middle grades for a course (D+'s, Cs and B−'s)—and using old traditional methods of assessment, that is statistically the way grades played out. Under the traditional grading philosophy, most students *were expected* to become just average academically, with a smaller percentage falling above and below that standard. If the apex of the bell curve—meaning the majority of student grades—fell in the C+/B− range, the teacher

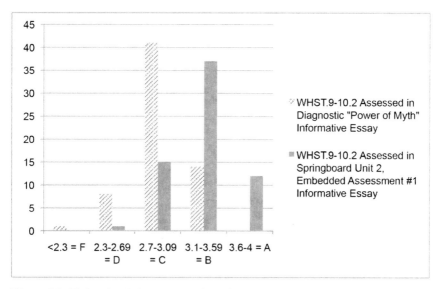

Figure 8.3. High school class scores for informative/explanatory essay-writing skills

was satisfied. There needed to be fewer As and usually some Fs and Ds. The teacher expected winners and losers.

The focus of standards-based grading, however, runs contrary to traditional acceptable classroom outcomes. Rather than accept the concept of winners and losers, the focus for a standards-based classroom is on bringing all students to "meet standard" and to get as many as possible to "exceed it." As is visible in figure 8.3, most students for the "Power of Myth" diagnostic assessments fell into the D to C range, with some getting Bs. Again, this was not a new task for students; they had written informative/explanatory essays before in previous grades. With the new grading term, though, came an expectation of a higher level of sophistication in writing. The students who received Bs and Cs in their essay-writing skills the previous year would now be getting Ds and Cs with the new term. Those who received As the previous year may start out receiving Bs. With continual practice, plentiful formative feedback, and further assessment, the majority of students move to the B and A range. Rather than a "bell curve" forming around the C grades, scores fall heavily in the upper grades to form a "J curve."

Again, the J curve represents a profound change in teaching philosophy. No longer is failure considered a normal classroom outcome. The goal is to get all students to standard and to push as many as possible beyond. No longer are substandard grades of D or F acceptable, although they may still occur. No longer do teachers need to feel uncomfortable with a large number of As if a large group of students are exceeding standard for their course work. Note: This is not grade inflation. These scores in the J curve represent a bump in skills and conceptual understanding based on better teaching strategies.

The march toward this J curve can often be a slow one, though, with scores not reaching a J shape until late in the term if the skills or concepts are difficult to achieve. If students get plentiful feedback (the key to academic growth in a traditional or a standards-based classroom) and assistance focused on meeting standards, though, a J curve should eventually emerge. If the course work is taught well and the criteria appropriately normed, the vast majority of students should meet or exceed course standard by the end of the term.

While this opportunity to score higher will appeal to students, they may at first become frustrated when their first attempts do not receive the scores they believe they deserve. Stripped of the padding that comes from rewarding work ethic (turning in large numbers of assignments) and extra-credit points, students may suddenly experience an honest assessment of their skill level or conceptual understanding. If final grades are based on "clear and convincing evidence" of students' understanding or skill level at grading time, though, students' grades will recover as they work toward higher scores. This strong work ethic, though, is essential to their academic growth and becomes funneled into sharpening skills and deepening understanding (as opposed to just churning out extraneous work), which are the new basis for the grades.

Educating students and parents or guardians to this new grading model is essential. For teachers and administrators, the first open house of the year is an excellent place to educate parents. For students, the new expectations need to be made clear at the beginning of the grading term and reinforced each time assessments are returned.

Not surprisingly, getting parents or guardians to buy into basing scores on understandable standards and assigning grades that acknowledge growth are easy sells. It just needs to be done before the parents are caught off guard by lower than normal grades. The parent or guardian has their student's best interest in mind. When scores are assigned for worthwhile standards that students know and can articulate and averaging scores is abandoned in place of a system that actually rewards growth, parents and guardians can clearly see that these are in the best interest of their students.

The truth is that most adults, sometime in their lives, have been victims of ambiguous tests and have seen grades ravaged by the averaging of scores. The fact that the scores students receive for good work in December is dragged down by the work of lesser quality they completed in September simply seems unjust, when one thinks about it. This simply is not a good way to evaluate students. Most parents will welcome the change since it benefits their child.

A shift to standards-based assessment, however, reorients the teacher as well. After experiencing the shift to basing scores solely on academic performance, reviewing old grading practices can almost become uncomfortable. Seeing a large number of As and Bs very early in the terms reveals that grades were not based largely on standards that assess what students know or can do by the end of a term. How can a large number of students achieve academic excellence so early unless course expectations were too low or grades were not based on standards (but on the amount of work completed)?

Over the course of a term, though, students' grades in the standards-based grade book look like boats buoyed by a slow rising tide. At the beginning of the term, grades may be on the low side since skills and conceptual understanding, for most students, are still emerging. But as the term progresses and students benefit from solid instruction and plentiful descriptive feedback, scores drifts upward. As the term progresses, a J curve slowly appears as most students meet or exceed standards for the course.

* * *

For students to be empowered for excellence, they need to know how their efforts directly determine the outcome of their grades. This requires transparency in the grading process. Students need to be able to analyze their scores and determine where extra efforts should be applied to get the grades they desire. Students need to be able to recognize the rewards of their labor by viewing the growth in scores organized around standards. These students also need to see that their efforts will be rewarded with grades that honor growth—they won't be dragged backward by the scores of their initial efforts.

When it comes to achieving a desirable grade, students need to see the manifestation of that most empowering of statements: you are in control of your destiny. By empowering students to take control of their futures, excellence is empowered as well.

Shift 9

Channel the Desire for Improvement

For all of Mrs. Westerman's firmness, she does believe in giving students a chance to improve their scores. Every other week, students are assigned to check the media for a current event and bring a report back to class on what they found. Students can choose to present their reports to the class for extra credit. Further, extra credit can be earned for attending outside lectures at local colleges that relate to U.S. affairs, viewing movies and videos based on historical events, and completing public service for such activities as volunteering in local homeless shelters and participating in canned-food drives. Some of Mrs. Westerman's top students have class grades above 100 percent of the points possible for the basic course.

One of the most challenging parts of teaching is dealing with students who truly desire a grade higher than their measured level of academic achievement. Whether these students are chasing higher GPAs, trying to please their parents, or simply believing themselves worthy of a better grade, it is extremely hard to turn these young people away when they desire something better for themselves. Perhaps teachers shouldn't.

In the traditional classroom, students who have fallen behind or want to take their grade to the next level often request extra-credit work. At its heart, extra credit is a concept where students complete work beyond what is considered the normal scope of assignments in order to receive more points that result in a higher grade.

Essentially, extra credit can be a helpful method of allowing students to strive for higher grades. Teachers have doled out extra-credit points to students for very worthy efforts: attending movies or lectures that relate to class, doing extra homework that may prove beneficial, and so forth. When students have desired to boost their grades, extra credit was one way to remediate the effects of a system of averaging scores.

One problem with extra credit, though, is that academic grades can become boosted by the activities that have nothing to do with the course at hand. Extra-credit points have been granted for participation in canned-food drives and school spirit events. In one math class, bathroom passes, allotted at the beginning of the term, could be returned unused at the semester's end for extra-credit points. This is a true story. Imagine this: a grade that guaranteed admission to a major university was achieved due to a sound and solid bladder.

Another problem with extra credit is that at its heart it contradicts the concept of standards-based grading, the assessment method advocated in this book. In traditional grading, students amass points and their final total divided by the number possible is what determines the grade. The students' duty is to work to amass points. Extra credit allows them to continue amassing points beyond the scope of what they have accrued for required assignments, projects, and assessments. It's like picking up overtime pay to pad the paycheck. Listen to students in a classroom. Students talk about having, say, 102 percent in one of their classes, for example. If grades are a measurement of student achievement, how does one end up achieving more than what should be possible? Yet, extra credit is a very accepted activity.

In a standards-based environment, students' skills and conceptual understanding are measured against a fixed set of values. The points that end up in the grade book are not really payment for the level of work completed on a test or assignment. The points given are a measurement tool somewhat like a ruler. A 2 on a 4-point scale for an assignment, for example, is a measurement of how close a student is to meeting the standard for that activity.

Say, for example, parents were to hand out an allowance that is tied to their children's ability to complete three home tasks: keeping their room tidy, cleaning up after a meal, and weeding the garden. The money that the kids receive each week would be based on the quality of the work being done. If the children wanted more allowance, they would be more mindful of the three tasks assigned to them. When the children fell short of the expectations for these activities, they would receive less allowance. Basing pay for performance would prompt a discussion about what the kids could do to improve their chores and, as a result, raise their allowance. It would not be wise for parents to allow the children to do extra side tasks to make up the difference if they were paid less due to the tasks being done improperly. This would defeat the emphasis on making improvements on the three tasks assigned. If the children want a more sizable allowance, they would need to focus on doing a better job on the chores already given them.

Likewise, if teachers want to empower excellence in their students, they need to keep the focus on mastering the standards that measure solid academic growth. This means that the concept of extra-credit efforts needs to be revised.

If students want to pour extra energies into improving their grades, encourage them to do it. The best way, though, is to have students focus on improving their scores on class standards. Students can return to their score sheets or the online grade book and choose standards where they seek improvement. Next, give them the guidance where they can work on their own to improve their skills and/or conceptual understanding. If students prove they have improved their skills or knowledge, use the "extra-credit" score to overwrite the lesser one. With this method, students apply their energies to becoming better at skills and conceptual understanding (O'Connor 2007, 31–35).

When students come to know the class standards for success, they also come to understand where they are in their skills and understandings and what they need to do well. They come to know where they need to apply their efforts for a better grade.

When students know their scores early in the term, they can see where they need to apply extra efforts to get the grades they desire. That is the focus of shift 8, to make sure that scores are communicated clearly so that students have the insight about where best to apply their efforts to get the grades they desire.

Obviously, allowing all students to challenge their grade for every standard would be a logistical nightmare. However, a well-organized grade book should reveal areas where students, if they apply extra effort, could improve select scores and therefore have a chance at a higher grade.

While it may be impractical late in the grading term for all students to have access to an opportunity to raise *all* their scores, certainly it is manageable to allow those students on the cusp of a better grade to apply their "extra-credit" efforts to a key standard or two, which if raised, would boost them to a higher grade. From a logistical sense, perhaps only those students on the "bubble"—at a C+ and close to a B−, for example—should be given this opportunity.

If teachers adopt the grading practices in this book, students will be afforded the opportunities to improve their scores by having numerous chances already to become better at a particular standard. When teachers "mine student data" and create grades based on the growth that has taken place, they are rewarding extra student effort, which is largely what extra-credit points are intended to do. Still, if after "mining data," a student's grade lies on the bubble, let students pour extra efforts into improving the scores on a standard or two that may be holding them back. In this case, "extra credit" translates into improved learning and empowers excellence since it gives students that final chance to get the grade they desire. This method builds optimism because it allows students another opportunity to control their fate and work toward the academic and professional future they envision.

In the end, grading policies should honor student academic growth. Students should be freed to achieve a higher level of academic progress without fear of punishment of the past. Teachers, too, begin looking at their students differently, focusing on what the student is doing right and rewarding it while looking at the places where they can improve their skills and conceptual understanding. And "extra credit" in the form of allowing students the opportunity to pull themselves over a grade bubble empowers excellence since efforts are directed at improving themselves academically. Employing these progressive grading policies empower students. These practices build optimism and direct students to pursue excellence.

Shift 10

Reflect, Revise, and Differentiate

Mrs. Westerman's scores for her latest quiz came in low. While class scores normally follow a bell curve, these scores for the majority of quizzes fell in the D range. An experienced teacher, Mrs. Westerman chalked up the lower scores to the fact that this class of juniors was a lower bunch than what she had had in past years. They do not pay as close of attention to her lectures. They frequently arrive to class with incomplete assignments. This was unfortunate, she thought. With a shrug, she started her next unit.

In the business world, when sales figures fall for a quarter, executives or business owners go hunting for a reason. A slight down tick may be written off to the variables of the marketplace and accepted for a short time, but a significant drop certainly sends businesses searching for the cause—and a determination to return to prosperity. Businesses cannot afford to see a continued slump in sales and afford to survive.

To a large degree, sales figures are an indicator of how well a business is functioning. Take restaurants, for example. A regular, robust business is an indicator of excellent service and products that customers believe are delicious and appropriately priced. A newly opened competitor may draw customers away in the short term, but a quality restaurant should rebound if the community can support multiple eateries. If not, the restaurant needs to make adjustments to survive, such as revising the menu or adopting more competitive pricing. A steady stream of customers is the sign of economic health. Low sales figures means it's time to make a change.

When sales slump, businesses scramble to adjust or evolve to survive, which they must. Further, though, effective businesses make changes based on the *confidence* that they can—through hard work, creativity, and appropriate strategies—alter an outcome in their favor. Effective businesses believe they can create an environment in which success can take place.

Scores and grades are, in a sense, classroom sales figures. They reflect to what degree students have "bought" the lessons "served" them and can show that they can apply important concepts and skills. While some educators debate this, the scores and grades in a grade book can be a powerful indicator of how successful they are in working with students in their classrooms. Good scores are a sign of successful teaching and learning, just as scores that fall short of meeting standard reflect that more work needs to be done with students. As in businesses, effective teachers make changes based on the *confidence* that they can—through hard work, creativity, and appropriate strategies—alter an outcome in their favor.

If teachers are to empower excellence, they need to provide students with the best instruction and learning environment in which to excel. A good measurement of this is students' scores. When grading is based on articulated, age-appropriate standards (in the K–12 Common Core State Standards, for example), an abundance of good scores for activities or assessments reflect successful lessons. When many students fall short of proficiency, the lessons and the learning activities are most likely to blame. Effective teachers use students' scores as their form of self-assessment as businesses judge their own performance through their sales figures.

For teachers who want to reflect on their performance and revise their practice, the grade book becomes an ideal tool for immediate feedback. If teachers want to empower excellence, they need to present to students the best possible learning experiences.

REFLECTING ON PRACTICE THROUGH STUDENT DATA

Having grade books organized by assessed standards (which were described in shift 8) allows teachers to not only assess student progress but also reflect on the effectiveness of their lessons. This grade book performs as an automobile dashboard, whose gauges measure the performance of a car. When a driver wants to measure the car's performance, he or she need only look to the dashboard. Grade books should be viewed the same way for the effectiveness of their lessons, teaching, and classroom performance.

First off, scores need to be calibrated against a fixed set of well-articulated standards. Next, the teacher needs to determine what score is a standard for success. In 4-point scales, that number is typically a 3. For this discussion, a 4-point scale will be used in the illustrations, with a 3 being the standard for minimum proficiency. A quick scan of scores for a set of students can often reveal how well the learning went:

3   2   3   4   3.5   3   4   3   4   2   3.5

The teacher concerned about getting students to a 3—or standard—notices that nine out of eleven students show proficiency or better in that assessment. The lesson(s) and teaching that preceded the assessment were effective with most students. Using this information, the teacher knows which two students are in need of additional assistance. (At this point, the teacher must differentiate instruction in some form to bring the remaining two students to standard.) When all scores are totaled together and the sum is divided by the number of scores available, the average (or mean) appears. The average for the above scores is 3.2.

Assuming, though, the average of scores reflects a good overview of the class can be misleading. The next set of scores shows a different outcome:

4   2   2   4   2   3.5   3.5   2   4   4   2

How students did on this assignment is foggier at first glance. There were a high numbers of 4s. The average or mean score for this set of scores is a 3, which means that the class, when scores were calculated together, met success for the assessment in a 4-point scale. Still, scattered among the good scores is a disconcerting number of 2s, which reflect emerging understanding. To decipher these grades further, teachers need to compile statistics beyond the typical average or mean. Statistical measures known as mode and median allow teachers to dig deeper.

The median can be viewed as the narrow traffic divider in the middle of a roadway, which is also called a median. If scores are reorganized and laid out from lowest to highest, the median is the middle score. Let's return to the last set of scores reorganized from lowest to highest:

2   2   2   2   2   3.5   3.5   4   4   4   4

If the scores were laid out from lowest to highest, the median for this set of scores is a 3.5. That means that half the scores entered were above this and half were below. If only the median were calculated and considered, the lesson, statistically, still looks very good. The question to be asked, though, is how many of the scores fell below the standard of 3 since median will not determine that.

The mode—or the most common score registered—tells a different story for the last set of scores. While there were plenty of 4s, in this set of numbers, the most common score was a 2. In this case, there was a total of five 2s out of eleven scores entered. While over half the class scored a 3.5 or higher, nearly half the class did not. With nearly half the students not earning a 3 for this skill or concept, the lesson(s) or unit taught up until that time would be deemed short of success since a large number of students didn't meet basic proficiency on the assessment. The teacher would need to revise instructional practice the next time the lesson is used or the target taught. The teacher would also need to differentiate instruction for the students who received 2s.

Calculating mean, median, and mode can be time consuming. Help comes in the form of modern technology, though. Many electronic grade books can be set to determine the mean, median, and mode for both grades and scores. To judge whether a lesson was a success, the mean will give an idea of its overall performance, but it doesn't allow teachers to see how all students were doing as individuals in terms of progressing. Median and mode help flesh out that picture.

Whether or not the grade book calculates statistics, teachers can mentally tally the number of students who did do well on the activity or assessment as well as the number of those who did not. If these calculations do not register a high number of scores and grades at or above course standard for that activity (which implies most students are learning and apply skills and concepts), then some revision of lessons, or continued reteaching, is necessary. Essentially, the students' scores become a reflection on the lesson(s) taught.

A well-organized grade book should communicate two things:

• How well individual students are doing. For students not meeting standard, this means continued work with them to bring all students to success.
• How well individual lessons or activities functioned. If the majority of students do well, the lesson or unit can be deemed a success. If scores are low when looking at mean, median, or mode, this is a sign that the lesson (or unit to date) was less than effective; the assessment was faulty; it was inappropriately calibrated for the class; or it is early in the grading period when scores tend to be lower as students strive to meet standard. More whole class work may be needed.

In short, a grade book should be an instrument that speaks to educators and informs their practice. It should be an instrument that acts as a dashboard to gauge class progress—and to determine if lessons need to be retaught or instruction individualized or differentiated.

Essentially, the goal of every classroom is to bring *all* students to proficiency. This will result in rejection of the traditional bell curve in grading since failure is no longer considered inevitable. Rather than a bell curve—with its acceptance of success and failure—a J curve appears, where more students end up with grades that reflect "proficiency" or "exceeds proficiency." To quote Gene Kranz's memorable line from the movie *Apollo 13* (1995), "Failure is not an option." Empowering excellence in students means becoming intolerant of failure.

A transformation takes place in teachers and their practice when they evolve from seeing a grade book as a final depository for scores and come to mine it for the data it contains. When viewed as a reflective resource, the grade book reveals which whole-class lessons went well and which didn't. Having an occasional lesson fall short of expectations is not necessarily reflective of teacher proficiency. Creative, exemplary teachers strive to push the envelope with their students. On occasion, efforts fall short, for example, when a creative lesson, despite its intent, doesn't meet the mark. Students fail to connect to the lesson or don't understand the learning. When this happens, teachers work to revise the lesson if resurrecting it has merit. Perhaps the concept or skill simply needs to be taught again but differently if normally proficient students in abundant numbers fall short of standard.

Simply, effective teachers use students' scores as their form of sales figures. Educators use their scores to determine "successful" learning in a classroom. For the teachers committed to all students meeting standard, scores in the grade book allow them to focus in, to individualize, and to differentiate instruction, thus empowering the students to pursue excellence.

Apply Formative Feedback Liberally

It takes time to create excellence. If it could be done more quickly, more people would do it.

—John Wooden, legendary college basketball coach

Mrs. Westerman has 140 students and believes in the concept of feedback. Since all her classes are normally full or close to full, she gives her students feedback suggestions but in a whole-group setting. She believes that essay tests are far superior to multiple-choice tests as a means of assessment. To improve students' writing and thinking skills, she allows herself a couple of comments per paper that she expects students to read and apply to their next essay tests, but she does not have the time to talk to students individually about their work.

So far, this book has covered a progressive means of assessment, which allows students to benefit from the growth that has taken place in their learning, and the support structures—both pedagogically and emotionally—that need to be in place for students to grow. What is missing, though, is a discussion of the fertilizer in which all of this will flourish: rich applications of formative, descriptive feedback.

The feedback largely given so far has come in the form of an assessed grade or score against a given standard. This scoring is completed at the end of the activity. Assessment expert Rick Stiggins refers to this as *assessment of learning*, or a postmortem since the assessment and comments come after the learning has been completed (2007, 31).

While assessment *of* learning carries great weight in our education culture, it often does little to impact learning. "As uncomfortable as the idea might seem," Wormeli in *Fair Isn't Always Equal* writes, "we have to accept the fact that summative grades as we now use them have little pedagogical use" (2006, 90). Basically, unless students are given multiple opportunities to improve on a skill or their conceptual understanding (as is advocated in this book), comments on papers are "after the fact." Unless teachers insist on some form of revision in which these comments are addressed, the chances of them being applied in the future are very slim. For this reason, this type of feedback is referred to as assessment *of* learning since it is a measurement and commentary at the end of the activity of what has already taken place.

Rich and abundant feedback given during the activity is the foundation for student growth and possibly the single most important element in class-room success. Stiggins refers to this as *assessment for learning* due to its potential to impact student growth (2007, 31). "Descriptive feedback points out to the students their work's strengths and weaknesses before it is too late—before the final grade—and models the kind of thinking we want them to do themselves about their work," Stiggins writes (2007, 236).

This formative feedback is rich in its content; it builds skills and strength-ens conceptual understanding. This feedback can come directly from, but is not limited to, the following sources:

- Teacher commentary: This feedback comes in the form of direct sugges-tions and could be written or oral. This may also come in the form of probing questions that are used to redirect students' efforts and/or under-standing.
- Student commentary: Peer commentary can be particularly powerful since it is often well accepted. Peers too can use probing questions to redirect efforts and/or understanding.
- Self-reflection: When teachers are intentional about the use of rubrics, checklists, scaffolds, and models, students themselves can discover where their efforts fall short and what can be done to improve the final outcome. This is particularly powerful since these efforts at self-improvement set the stage for similar efforts in adult life.

Mark Barnes, in his book *Role Reversal*, advocates a four-part approach to feedback, which he calls SE2R (Summarize, Explain, Redirect, and Re-submit). According to Barnes, "Effective narrative feedback should always *summarize* and *explain* what a student has accomplished, based on the activ-ity or project guidelines. If the learning outcome is mastered, then the feed-back will end with these two components of the SE2R system. If further learning is required, then the student will be *redirected* to prior instruction and then *resubmit* the work for teacher evaluation" (2013, 74).

Barnes in his book advocates an online component to teaching, so his feedback would come in the form of written commentary on a blog or web page—or oral commentary when dealing with a student in person. In a brick-

and-mortar setting, this feedback would be written on student work and/or delivered orally. Either way, teachers, in the first two key components, summarize what they see in terms of the skill development or the conceptual understanding that the activity is trying to meet. Next, educators explain how the work is meeting that standard for that skill or concept. If the student work meets standard, the teacher lets them know what they did and why it was done correctly. If not, suggestions are made to move the student work toward the learning targets for that lesson. All written feedback should be accompanied by an oral explanation of it. *Summarize* and *explain* are powerful since they affirm student effort by telling them precisely what they are doing correctly.

Unlike the generic "good job" that many teachers may scrawl across the paper, good feedback is specific and objective. Barnes continues, "The key to successful feedback is to remain as objective as possible. It's okay to tell a child that her work is 'nicely done' but only after a detailed summary and explanation have been provided" (2013, 74).

If a student falls short of meeting the learning target for the activity, Barnes advocates *redirecting* and *resubmitting* as part of SE2R. In this case, the formative feedback redirects the student toward better skill development or understanding. After improvements or revisions have been made, students resubmit their work for a second round of assessment to make sure that they are meeting the learning target.

Logistically, teachers should never spend too much time dispensing formative feedback beyond *summarize* and *explain* unless the students *will* apply it in the immediate future. All too often, teachers spend hours writing suggestions on papers only to see many of them tossed in the wastebasket or recycle bin. When teachers take the time to provide feedback, there needs to be a direct application to future learning, otherwise the commentary becomes *assessment of learning* as opposed to *assessment for learning*. While writing comments may feel good for teachers (writing some comment is deeply engrained in most of us), this practice is unproductive. Most of the time, students read the comments but don't apply them unless there is a follow-up opportunity to do so.

Feedback should be directed individually to students, or if there is a common problem among a number of students, they can be grouped together for a common presentation and discussion. Feedback is then followed by some form of activity to hold students accountable for its application.

Key to effective descriptive feedback is that it must be focused and limited. Stiggins writes,

> If we are focusing on one trait and one trait at a time, we only need to give descriptive feedback on that one trait. This has the effect of narrowing the scope of work for both the teacher and the student. With struggling students,

we can show them they do indeed know some things and we can limit the things they need to work on at one time to a less daunting, more manageable number. (Stiggins et al., 2007, 236)

One of the great misunderstandings of formative, descriptive feedback is that it needs to be cumbersome. Teachers can move among working students, scan a problem or a project, and either make a descriptive comment or direct a probing question to confirm or redirect thinking. None of this needs to be time consuming, nor does it need to be recorded in the grade book. Descriptive assessment for learning is simply designed to help students learn.

What makes the workshop model so successful is the component of abundant formative feedback. In the workshop model, learning is set in bite-sized chunks and is applied immediately. While students work in class, the teacher circulates among the desks viewing student efforts and giving individual feedback on the spot. Rather than collect the activity, make commentary later, and then return it to the students, the teacher circulating in the classroom gives as much feedback as time allows. If not all students are reached, the teacher gets to the remaining students during the next work session. In its simplest function, the workshop model is a container for appropriate and abundant formative feedback.

Previously in this book, statistical models of the bell curve and the J curve were discussed. A bell curve is a classic example of a classroom low on formative feedback: a very few "get it" and have the top scores; most students "sort of get it" and form the bubble of the statistical model. On the other hand, abundant formative feedback is responsible for the statistical J curve. As feedback is applied liberally, more students learn, and as a result, scores and grades become higher, creating the *J* effect when grades are plotted. This is not grade inflation. These scores reflect actual student growth in skills and conceptual understanding.

The spirit in which the formative feedback is given can be as impactful as the information delivered itself. Simply, if done correctly, formative feedback significantly honors the humanity of the student. Too often, teachers are viewed as being "above" students. The proper delivery of formative feedback can level this relationship and transform the teacher into a coach in students' lives. How?

Meet at the students' eye level. This could mean sitting with a group of students at a desk, inviting them to have a seat in a chair by the teacher's desk, or kneeling at their desks—just don't stand above them and literally talk down to them. Dispense commentary eye to eye, watching their facial expressions to make sure the ideas are well received. Looks of confusion are signs that the feedback is not being adequately understood. While sufficient space is necessary to keep relations appropriate and professional, physical proximity and open body postures are an important component for formative feedback since they facilitate the messages being received. Make sure to compliment students and tell them what is great about their work before making suggestions or redirecting. Everyone flourishes with positive comments.

Teacher feedback should be a case of "gradual release of responsibility" where assessment duties are slowly being handed over to students. As students become more knowledgeable with rubrics, models, and grading standards, they should start assuming more responsibilities for their own growth. Good, honest self-reflection is a form of formative assessment—teachers should take great efforts to get students to summarize their own knowledge and apply it in the form of self-assessment. Students should also be able to reflect on a self-assessment version of Richard DuFour's four questions from *Learning by Doing: A Handbook for Professional Learning Communities at Work* (2010, 28):

- What have I learned?
- How do I know that I have learned it?
- What don't I know that I need to know?
- What do I need to do next now that I have learned it?

Basically, life is a process of self-education. As a result, the skill of self-assessment becomes a process that students can use their lives through.

Further, teachers should employ peer assessment whenever possible. Rubrics, models, and standards become more relevant and understandable when students must apply this knowledge to other students' work. And students often accept feedback more openly from their peers. While peer reflection and editing at times may not be as strong or precise at teacher feedback, it nevertheless provides further formative feedback upon which students can learn. These peer evaluations are best related orally to the student and written on their schoolwork to be remembered during the revision process or further attempts at mastering a concept.

Teachers enter the classroom with a great bank of skills and conceptual understanding. Students are in need of these skills and concepts if they are to be successful in adult life. The transfer of this knowledge and understanding is the basis of teaching, and formative feedback is one of teaching's most powerful tools to accomplish this.

Shift 12

Celebrate Success

After she has corrected her essay tests, Mrs. Westerman organizes them from worst scores to best scores before she hands them out. This is her own form of self-assessment to see how well the students learn the content. In class, this allows for a sense of anticipation. The longer the student waits as she hands back scored tests, the greater the anticipation of a good grade and therefore a celebration for those who strive for an excellent grade. Unfortunately, Mrs. Westerman doesn't notice that the students who receive the first tests cringe as their papers are drawn from the top of the stack. She just enjoys the looks of pleasure of students who have worked hard and are receiving a top score.

There is a saying: success breeds success. Too often in classrooms, though, the only success that is recognized is a good grade written across the top of an essay, a test, or a report. When this is the case, only the top students receive the accolades for a job well done. Unfortunately, the majority of students spend their time in classrooms and receive little recognition for a job well done. If teachers ever feel underappreciated, students most likely feel even more so. Too often good efforts on students' parts end not with a bang but with a whimper.

How does a teacher go about recognizing and honoring excellence? The easiest and most direct form of accolade comes in the form of positive formative feedback during *summarize* and *explain*, referred to in the last chapter. When looking at student work, find that which is positive and acknowledge it. Too often, comments on papers record what needs to be done for improvement, which can be deflating for those students who have worked their hearts out on an activity. Make sure the comment is both objective and specific so the students know well what is being celebrated in their work. In fact, sandwich what needs to be done in between two comments about what is going well in the students' work. Every student has something he or she can improve on, but why not stress the progress that has been made?

The key to the shift in thinking is recognizing that excellence is a relative term. At any given time, a classroom is filled with students having a wide range of skills and conceptual understanding. Teachers should acknowledge academic improvement relative to the growth that has taken place in each student, not against some fixed standard for all students. When looking at student work, always find and acknowledge something that is going right. Let every student share in a bounty of positive comments.

To keep a focus on academic progress, teachers should regularly sit down with students, go over their scores and grades, and celebrate their success. A grade book where scores are organized around standards allows for discussion of progress being made. This is a time for the teacher and the student to dialogue about where scores began, students' efforts to improve their grades, and how those efforts paid off. In terms of optimism, this is the place to show many student how "bad events" are temporary and how they have the power, through hard work and study, to improve their grades. This is the time for students to take internal responsibility for their success. This lesson about controlling one's destiny transcends the classroom and has positive consequences for their lives as adults. Students become empowered to achieve excellence.

Let classroom walls and hallways be cluttered with students' accomplishments. When teachers have students create nonliteral interpretation or understanding—a great way to really know what students do and do not understand—classroom walls become an appropriate place to acknowledge these colorful diagrams and artistic representations. Further, students who find academics challenging may have exceptional artistic skills. Posting their work shows that value is placed and acknowledged on what they do well.

When students do exemplary work, ask for copies to be used as models for future study. Since models are an extremely effective way to teach, make copies of them and place them in folders for future study. Teachers should continually gather examples of exemplary work for future study in class. Asking students for copies of their best work is to pay them a high compliment—and they recognize it.

Even though all student work may not be exemplary, be specific in commentary about what makes the assignment, assessment, or project completed good work. The feedback should be regarding what constitutes excellence in the work completed.

When people achieve or make a contribution in our culture, we "give it up" for them in the form of applause. When students have done exceptional work in class or made some great stride in their academics, why not acknowledge these efforts publicly and ask the class for a round of applause on the students' behalf? When a class does well, walk among students giving "high fives"—and watch the energy level in the classroom soar.

Effective teachers are very proactive in contacting parents when students are failing or not meeting standards for their classes. Why not make a positive phone call when students display excellence or make a major stride in their skills? Too often, parents are only contacted when there is something going wrong at school. A phone call home when academics are going well can be an extremely powerful form of affirmation.

Literacy fairs and science fairs are a great way of displaying students' best efforts. One Spokane elementary school fills its gymnasium yearly with artifacts of students' best literacy efforts. Tables are filled with notebooks of students' writing and illustrations, and the walls are covered with students' artistic representations. Parents, the community, and school administrators are invited to come and view the students' work, but those who benefit are the students who are being acknowledged for their hard work.

Publishing is an excellent way to celebrate success. Have students share final published works in small groups and have the group members write and share specific, positive comments. Student work can be loaded up into a blog or public website for positive commentary—just omit the last name for personal safety's sake. Cornelius Minor, a New York City middle school teacher and instructor for the Columbia University's Summer Writing Institute, posts student work in delicatessens and Laundromats—two places where people of all ages congregate and have time to observe exemplary efforts.

To celebrate success, teachers need to undergo a shift in their thinking: away from looking for faults in student work and toward what is going right. By acknowledging excellence in all its forms and at all its relative levels, while improving in needed areas, teachers empower students to pursue it more. Remember, success breeds success, so acknowledge it whenever possible. Make every effort to end a lesson or exhibition with a bang of some sort—a positive statement or acknowledgment of a job well done. While nothing breeds success like success, few things empower the pursuit of excellence more than acknowledgment of a job well done.

Closing

At its heart, empowering excellence is about releasing the great potential that lies within students. Effective practitioners are guided by a vision of what can be, and they empower students to undertake a transformational learning process that will benefit them for a lifetime. Essentially, teachers, using a variety of instructional methodologies, seek to liberate the potential that lies within each student.

While this book delves deeply into assessment methods and teaching theory, educators need to establish an important balance in their classrooms and be diligent on three fronts. Course standards and learning targets become the stars by which we navigate our practice, but they are neither the journey nor the destination. The journey involves robust and engaging content and curriculum. The destination is well-rounded students and critical-thinking individuals who function well in their professional and personal lives and have high levels of appreciation for our world.

Empowering excellence involves educators setting in motion essential skills, conceptual understanding, and inner beliefs that will benefit students for a lifetime.

References

America's Promise Alliance. "Dropout Rate Crisis." 2013. Accessed January 3, 2014.http://www.americaspromise.org/Our-Work/Grad-Nation/Dropout-Facts.aspx.

Apollo 13. Directed by Ron Howard. Universal City, CA: Universal Pictures, 1995.

Barnes, Mark. *Role Reversal: Achieving Uncommonly Excellent Results in the Student-Centered Classroom.* Alexandria, VA: Association for Supervision and Curriculum Development, 2013.

Campbell, Joseph. *The Power of Myth.* New York: Doubleday, 1988.

"Common Core State Standards Initiative: Preparing American's Students for College and Career." 2012. Accessed January 3, 2014. http://www.corestandards.org/ELA-Literacy.

Covey, Stephen R. *The Seven Habits of Highly Effective People.* First Fireside ed. New York: Simon & Schuster, 1990.

Daisley, Patrick. January 9, 2014.

DuFour, Richard, Rebecca DuFour, Robert Eaker, and Thomas Many. *Learning by Doing: A Handbook for Professional Learning Communities at Work.* 2nd ed. Bloomington, IN: Solution Tree Press, 2010.

Dweck, Carol S. *Mindset: The New Psychology of Success.* New York: Ballantine Books, 2008.

Guskey, Thomas R., and Jane M. Bailey. *Developing Grading and Reporting Systems for Student Learning.* Thousand Oaks, CA: Corwin Press, 2001.

Hoerr, Thomas R. *Fostering Grit: How Do I Prepare My Students for the Real World?* Alexandria, VA: Association for Supervision and Curriculum Development, 2013.

Lee, Harper. *To Kill a Mockingbird.* New York: Warner Books, 1982.

O'Connor, Ken. *How to Grade for Learning: Linking Grades to Standards.* Thousand Oaks, CA: Corwin Press, 2002.

———. *A Repair Kit for Grading: 15 Fixes for Broken Grades.* Portland, OR: Educational Testing Service, 2007.

Powell, Erik. January 15, 2014.

Prosser, Ronald. March 10, 2014.

Seligman, Martin E. P. *Learned Optimism.* New York: Pocket Books, 1991.

Stiggins, Richard J., Judith A. Arter, Jan Chappuis, and Stephen Chappuis. *Classroom Assessment for Student Learning: Doing It Right—Using It Well.* Portland, OR: Educational Testing Service, 2007.

Tomlinson, Carol Ann, and Jay McTighe. *Integrating Differentiated Instruction and Understanding by Design*. Alexandria, VA: Association for Supervision and Curriculum Development, 2006.

Wiggins, Grant, and Jay McTighe. *Understanding by Design*. Expanded 2nd ed. Alexandria, VA: Association for Supervision and Curriculum Development, 2005.

Wong, Harry. *First Days of School*. Mountain View, CA: Wong and Wong Productions, 2009.

Wormeli, Rick. *Fair Isn't Always Equal: Assessing and Grading in the Differentiated Classroom*. Portland, ME: Stenhouse Publishers, 2006.

Index

About the Author

Jeff Halstead brings a wealth of experience to the topic of effective classroom instruction and assessment. A National Board–certified teacher and staff developer, he has spent over twenty years in the classroom, teaching English, journalism, and social studies. He served as a trainer, leader, and curriculum designer for the Teacher Leadership Project, which trained over 3,500 Washington State educators in the use of instructional technology. In Spokane public schools, he helped create an intensive professional-development program entitled Building the Capacity for Leadership in Technology, which trained over four hundred teachers to infuse instructional technology into best-teaching practices. He has been a course developer and trainer for the Washington Education Association's JumpStart Innovators program. In addition, Halstead has designed and taught virtual-learning courses, served as a Washington State University facilitator for National Board candidates, and led graduate-level education classes. He has presented at regional conferences and at workshops around the United States. Halstead received his bachelor's degree in English and his master's degree in education from Whitworth University. His work has been featured in major newspapers, as well as regional and national magazines. He lives with his family and dogs in Spokane, Washington. Visit his website at http://www.thenewpedagogy.com/. He can be contacted via e-mail at NavNewPedagogy@aol.com.

CPSIA information can be obtained at www.ICGtesting.com
Printed in the USA
BVOW07s0514260614

357404BV00001B/2/P